PUERTO RICO
TO THE
WHITE HOUSE

A MEMOIR OF
POSSIBILITIES
AND PERSISTENCE

Jacob Lozada, PhD

Produced by Inksnatcher.com.

Printed in the United States of America.

LCCN record available at https://lccn.loc.gov/Library of Congress Cataloging-in-Publication Data

Names: Lozada, Jacob, author
Title: Puerto Rico to the White House: A Memoir of Possibilities and Persistence / Jacob Lozada

Subjects: | BIOGRAPHY & AUTOBIOGRAPHY / Hispanic & Latino. BIOGRAPHY & AUTOBIOGRAPHY / Military. BIOGRAPHY & AUTOBIOGRAPHY / Cultural & Regional

Description: First edition. | Boricua Legacy Books, 2025. | Summary: "From Puerto Rican public housing to the halls of the White House, Jacob Lozada's memoir is a powerful testament to faith, perseverance, and the life-changing impact of service." —Provided by publisher.

Identifiers: LCCN 2025913470 | 979-8-9992376-0-6 (paperback) | 979-8-9992376-1-3 (hardback) | 979-8-9992376-2-0 (e-book)

Unless otherwise stated, all Scripture quotations are from the King James Version of the Bible, public domain.

For information about special discounts for bulk purchases, please contact the author at jacoblozada052@gmail.com.

To my parents, Juan Lozada and Clotilde Pereira,
who instilled in me the values of hard work,
perseverance, and accountability.

CONTENTS

LIST OF IMAGES

PROLOGUE

When I served on the AARP Board of Directors, I was invited by a group of young employees to talk about mentoring. During the Q&A period, a young Hispanic asked, "Dr. Lozada, do you believe in the American Dream?"

I pointed at myself and said, "Yes, look at me!"

Not a day goes by that I don't think about my humble beginnings in public housing in Puerto Rico, my careers in the U.S. Army and the private sector, my appointments by two presidents, and my service in the not-for-profit sector.

I am eighty years old now, and the memories of the roads I have traveled and the people I have met are still alive. Also alive are the many challenges and difficulties I faced mastering a language (English) different from my own (Spanish), assimilating into a different culture, and working harder than others to succeed.

Luckily, I live in a country where a young Puerto Rican kid—through hard work, determination, and initiative—can overcome challenges and disappointments, achieve success, and accomplish his aspirations. In this respect, I am most grateful.

Having loving but tough parents made a big difference in my life. They instilled in me the desire to be the best, to be a positive role model, and to help others. Doing my best and never quitting were the most important lessons my mom taught me. She often told me, "I am raising you to be strong and independent. Don't blame others. Don't ever assume a victim mentality."

These traits define me as I journey through life.

INTRODUCTION

Invictus

It matters not how strait the gate,
How charged with punishments the scroll,
I am the master of my fate,
I am the captain of my soul.

William Ernest Henley

On March 18, 2018, I received a letter from the chairman of the Ellis Island Honors Society, informing me that he and the board of directors had selected me to receive the 2018 Ellis Island Medal of Honor. Medals would be presented to 100 distinguished Americans during a ceremony on Ellis Island. I was nominated for this prestigious award by Dr. Victor S. Wahby, director of the Medical Musical Group Chorale and Symphony Orchestra. I was at a loss for words when I was informed of my nomination and quickly reached out to Dr. Wahby to express my appreciation.

The 2018 Medal Yearbook describes the award as "a symbol of the diversity of our nation's people. It is from this diversity that the United States is still a beacon of hope for so many, and the greatest democracy the world has ever known."[1] Many notable individuals have received the Ellis Island Medal of Honor, including former New York City Mayor Rudolph Giuliani, Dr. Deepak Chopra, President Donald J. Trump, Muhammad Ali, comedian Bob Hope, former President Ronald Reagan, and Cuban American singer Gloria Estefan.

In 2018, former football star Franco Harris, Puerto Rican actress and dancer Rita Moreno, Admiral Michael S. Rogers, and His Serene Highness Prince Albert II of Monaco received the award. As a recipient, it was humbling for me to be in such good company!

On Friday, May 11, I joined the awardees at a reception at The Wagner Hotel at Battery Park. Small cocktail tables covered with white tablecloths and flower arrangements filled the room. The red, white, and yellow flowers stood out against the tablecloths. In an adjacent room, a private dinner followed the reception. The evening concluded with several songs and dances by members of a Broadway theater troupe. Their rhythmic music and lively dances created a joyful and lively atmosphere.

I was overwhelmed by the evening's activities—they were well beyond my wildest expectations. Being in the company of so many influential dignitaries was equally impressive. I was on cloud nine!

The following evening, the medal recipients and their guests rode a ferry to Ellis Island. When we arrived, a military honor guard stood on either side of a red carpet that led us into the Registry Room, where millions of immigrants had passed through on their way to America. Trunks and pieces of luggage, Bibles and prayer books, family documents and handmade clothes and linens were on display.

The displays made me pause. I felt a weight in my chest as I thought about the many hardships these immigrants must have endured as they traveled across the oceans to America.

I was in awe of the sacrifices they must have made while traveling to America, not knowing what the future would hold and the challenges they would face in a strange and faraway land. As I thought about their journey, I couldn't help but reflect on my life and the challenges I had also faced moving from Puerto Rico to the U.S. mainland.

After a short reception, we entered a large banquet hall, which included tables with gold tablecloths and flower arrangements. I sat at table 72, not far from the stage.

After several short speeches and introductions, the master of ceremonies introduced a chorus of Soldiers from the 82nd Airborne Division from Fort Bragg, North Carolina. As a former military officer, their presence—and participation—was a special treat. Soon thereafter, the emcee began introducing awardees.

As I waited for my name to be called, I remembered my childhood in Puerto Rico and the sacrifices my parents made to ensure a good education for me. I thought of my mom's encouragement when she noticed my nervousness before delivering my high school graduation speech. I recalled redoubling my efforts to improve my English as a young officer in the U.S. Army. I was overwhelmed by being there, surrounded by so many celebrities—remembering my mom, her teachings, and her unyielding love.

I returned my attention to the stage, heard my name, and saw my photo on a large screen above the stage. Those sitting at adjacent tables immediately looked toward me.

The feelings of personal pride and satisfaction were overwhelming! As the emcee read my biography, I walked to the stage, where two young ladies placed a heavy medal—engraved with the Statue of Liberty—around my neck. I turned to the audience and the stage lights blinded me as I waited for photos. After acknowledging the thunderous applause, I returned to my seat.

After the ceremony, the ferry stopped in front of the Statue of Liberty and fireworks exploded. Bright lights and loud noises filled the sky. The sight of Lady Liberty surrounded by fireworks made me proud of living in our great nation and thankful for the opportunities America had given me. I couldn't help but be overtaken by overwhelming happiness and pride.

This book was not written to boast about my achievements. It's an example of what an individual can achieve with determination, discipline, and hard work. I hope that sharing my life path will motivate our nation's youth—especially our youth in Puerto Rico—to dream big, work hard, and apply the lessons I learned to achieve the American Dream. If by sharing my life's story I help just one person, my mission has been accomplished.

Jacob Lozada, PhD
Austin, Texas

CHAPTER 1

"SOMEONE FROM THE WHITE HOUSE IS CALLING YOU!"

GRAY CLOUDS FILLED THE SKY, AND THE TEMPERATURE dropped below forty degrees on Monday, January 15, 2001, when I arrived at the Electronic Data Systems (EDS) building in Herndon, Virginia. At the time, I worked as a management consultant—identifying consulting opportunities, authoring proposals, and managing projects. I enjoyed my job because it enabled me to help clients improve their organizations.

I'd been closely following the recent presidential election, in which George W. Bush had been elected president following an electoral fight, ultimately decided by the U.S. Supreme Court. The delay in deciding the election impacted the transition to the new administration. The time to identify, interview, and select qualified individuals to take over the reins of the federal government had been shortened from approximately four months to two. Former Secretary of Defense Richard B. Cheney led the Bush-Cheney presidential transition team.

While the transition team worked, a committee planned a series of inaugural galas to be held at various venues in the nation's capital. The galas transformed the city by bringing together thousands of campaign workers, political supporters, private sector leaders, government officials, and tourists.

1

Presidential Gala

I had never attended an inaugural gala but had heard they were exciting and worth experiencing at least once. Eager to join in the experience, I purchased tickets for the Hispanic Presidential Inaugural Gala to be held on Friday, January 19 at the Omni Shoreham Hotel.

Riding the metro train on a cold and rainy winter night was out of the question. Instead, I hired a taxi to take me to the hotel. Having private transportation to the gala proved to be an excellent idea because the traffic was almost unbearable as we rode into Washington, DC! A regular thirty-minute automobile drive from my home into the city had now turned into a long hour-and-a-half convoy with drivers zigzagging and aggressively competing for a few empty road lanes. As we traveled, I became increasingly annoyed by the traffic and questioned whether attending the gala was a good idea.

When I entered the hotel lobby, I identified Hispanic leaders from all sectors of society. I remember seeing former Governor Luis A. Ferré, Housing Secretary-Designate Mel Martínez, and musician and producer Emilio Estefan. Everyone wore formal attire. I wore my military awards and decorations on a black tuxedo.

As I stood at a check-in desk, a Hispanic gentleman stared at my medals and said, "Sir, thank you for your service. Which job are you getting in President Bush's team?" Stunned by the question, I explained that I was not being considered for a position in the incoming administration, and I was at the gala because I had been told that the experience was worthwhile.

The Omni was an elbow-to-elbow madhouse of activity. There were valets greeting guests at the hotel entrance, long lines of people standing in front of registration desks, and hotel staff swerving around answering questions and directing attendees to the different venues. It was true pandemonium!

The noise was deafening. Live bands played Mexican Mariachi music, Puerto Rican and Cuban salsa, and Brazilian samba tunes. The walls shook and vibrated with the beat of the music. People fought their way to the many bars and finger-food stations. It was so loud that I had to yell at the person next to me.

As I exchanged war stories with a former Army friend, a band played "Hail to the Chief." I turned my attention to the stage and saw President Bush and the First Lady waving and smiling no more than ten yards from where I stood! I was enthralled by being near the president—it was an event for which I was not mentally prepared.

The president greeted the attendees before dancing with the first lady to thunderous applause. After the short dance, they smiled, waved, and exited to visit other inaugural galas. I had never seen a president in person. Being a few steps away from the leader of the free world made me feel special and uniquely important. It was all very exciting!

Image 1. The author with Governor Luis A. Ferré at the 2001 Hispanic Presidential Inaugural Gala

The gala included speeches by Hispanic leaders as well as excellent performances by various artists. One of the main performances was carried out by an Argentine couple who danced several tangos. The audience was mesmerized by the beautiful music and the complicated steps of the dancers. Their stealthy cat-like movements, intricate footwork, and passionate dancing had everyone hypnotized. Their dancing was as good as the performances I had seen in Buenos Aires, years before.

As the evening progressed, I realized that the gala provided a great opportunity for networking. I had brought business cards with me, so I shared them with those I met. No doubt, a presidential inaugural gala was worth attending at least once!

Leaving the hotel was challenging. There were so many vehicles waiting to pick up passengers that my taxi driver could not get close to the hotel. I called and asked him to wait at his location, two long blocks away. As a cold rain washed over the city, I sprinted to the taxi. Panting and perspiring, I jumped into the warm vehicle.

BAD NEWS

A few days later, the environment at EDS changed when we learned the Government Consulting Services (GCS), where I worked, was going to be dissolved. We were shocked and angered by the unexpected news; our team was doing a great job supporting government clients. After the announcement, some consultants began pursuing job opportunities in private sector firms; others moved to different practices within the firm. I didn't want to move to a different firm, so I began to explore other job opportunities within EDS.

As the days went by, our GCS team started to shrink. What had been a tightly knit team was now a disparate group of individuals trying to figure out their future. With little information forthcoming, we felt abandoned and betrayed by corporation leadership.

Within this uncertain environment, I was hired into the EDS e-learning practice. This group developed web-based training for several clients, including the Ford Motor Company. I also co-led a training project in Argentina. In this role, I helped develop the training program and selected some of the topics to be taught.

The e-learning work was different. I had previously worked directly with clients and now had to work remotely. The e-learning practice was based in Detroit, but I continued to work in Herndon. The work was interesting, but I missed working with my former GCS teammates. For the first time in my professional career, I felt lonely and disconnected from my colleagues.

While I continued to adjust to my new normal, I considered applying for a leadership job in President Bush's administration. Working as a member of the president's leadership team would be the capstone to my twenty-seven-year career in the military followed by ten years in the private sector. I could leverage the experience I had gained—while representing Puerto Rico and the Hispanic community—at the highest levels of the federal government. I had always been attracted to public service, and a presidential appointment would be another opportunity to serve my country and give back.

The odds of landing an appointment were not in my favor. I had never been involved in partisan politics. In addition, I had neither moved in political circles nor actively campaigned in support of any local or national political candidates. These shortcomings didn't deter me. I pressed on, knowing that the new administration was looking to hire highly qualified individuals. I also felt that my professional experience and accomplishments improved my chances of being selected.

I told two people about my plan: Dr. Victor Wahby, director of the Medical Musical Group Chorale and Symphony Orchestra, and Dr. René Rodríguez, president of the Interamerican College of Physicians and Surgeons. They were both enthusiastic about my application. After consulting with my family and analyzing the pros and cons, I posted my resume on the president's transition team website and waited.

The cold January weather did not slow the pace at EDS. As I prepared to attend a morning staff meeting, I heard the quick steps of someone approaching my cubicle. Still focused on my work, a voice said, "Jake, someone is calling you on my telephone." I turned around and saw one of our executive assistants staring at me. I asked her to take the caller's name and telephone number so I could return the call later, but she said, "You need to take this phone call right now. Someone from the White House is calling you!"

I hurried down the hallway, not knowing what to think. *Who from the White House would be calling me*? I entered the executive assistant's office and picked up the phone. "Hello?"

"Are you Dr. Jacob Lozada?"

"Yes, sir."

"Dr. Lozada, I am calling from the Office of Presidential Personnel, and we want to talk to you. We would like to interview you this afternoon at 2 p.m. Report to the Northeast Gate of the White House, facing Pennsylvania Avenue, give the security guard your name and driver's license, and tell him or her that you have an appointment in the Office of Presidential Personnel. After you are cleared to enter, proceed to the right and into the West Wing of the White House."

I was overwhelmed by the call.

My heart was beating out of my chest.

I said very little, choosing instead to take detailed notes of the instructions given to me by the caller. Afraid my emotions would betray me, I didn't ask the caller any questions.

It was approximately 11 a.m. when the call ended. I was too rushed to eat a full lunch, so I forced myself to eat a quick chicken salad sandwich and headed home to change clothes before driving to the metro station. After changing into my best business suit, a neatly pressed white shirt, and a conservative necktie, my hands trembling as I tied the knot, I drove the ten minutes to the Vienna metro station.

After a few minutes on the metro train platform, I saw the bright lights of an approaching train. After the train stopped and passengers exited, I entered the first car. I looked up at the metro system map posted on the wall and quickly figured out that the closest station to the White House was McPherson Square.

My body dropped into the seat like a twenty-pound backpack, grateful for some support as I tried to foresee what was about to take place during my visit to the White House and my interview in the Office of Presidential Personnel.

Soon afterward a prerecorded voice announced, "Stand back, doors closing." The doors closed with a clunk and the train slowly moved forward. As we left the station and the train gained speed, the conductor—in a booming baritone voice—announced, "Welcome to Metro Train. This is the Orange Line to New Carrollton."

As I rode to the White House, I felt excited but somewhat nervous. I didn't know what to expect but felt confident because I had undergone several interviews in the private sector. During the trip, I reviewed the lessons I had learned about interviewing: be positive, listen carefully, be aware of your body language and tone of voice, and be brief and to the point.

I planned to arrive early so I could familiarize myself with the surroundings and get into my comfort zone.

CHAPTER 2

GROWING UP IN PUERTO RICO

I WAS BORN IN 1944 AND REARED IN SAN LORENZO, PUERTO Rico, in the eastern central region of the island.

When I was a child, San Lorenzo was an agricultural town. Surrounded by dark green hills and rolling pastures, it grew tobacco, sugar cane, and other products. In the following decades, many new residents moved to the town, attracted by its mild climate and proximity to San Juan (the capital of Puerto Rico).

MY DAD AND MOM MEET

Though my dad was born in Humacao and my mom on a coffee plantation in Guayama, they met by happenstance in San Lorenzo when my mom was eighteen and my dad was twenty-eight. According to my mom, they met when she was gathering water from a public faucet in *El Bosque* (The Forest), one of our poorest neighborhoods. Gathering water from public faucets was a common practice in those days because many homes in those neighborhoods did not have running water. Unfortunately, most did not have sewage systems either. My dad was instantly struck by my mom's beauty, so he initiated a conversation, a gesture she did not appreciate.

8

"I told him he should be ashamed, an old man flirting with a young girl like me," my mom, visibly annoyed, said. "I told him I knew his mother and was going to tell her."

My dad was a widower at twenty-eight, and his mother was the pastor of the local Pentecostal church. She was respected in our town and one of a handful of female Pentecostal church leaders on the island.

My mom's rebuke did not intimidate my dad—he was smitten!

My mom's life story was one of extreme difficulty, scarcity, and hardship. She never met her father, and when she was a child, her mom died of tuberculosis, a common disease in Puerto Rico in the 1930s. Her only sister also died of this dreaded disease at a very young age. It was a miracle my mom was not infected by her sister's disease, nor suffered the same fate.

Throughout her childhood, my mom never slept on a regular bed but on a shared mattress stuffed with dried banana leaves and laid on the bare floor. When my mom and her little sister turned their bodies around while they slept, the dry leaves sounded like *maracas* (a musical instrument that you shake, made from dried, hollow gourds filled with dry beans or pebbles). After her mother's and sister's deaths, my mom, having nowhere to go, ended up moving from house to house, living with several relatives while doing domestic work. My mom was a very strong and stoic woman—the only times I saw her cry were when she shared this part of her difficult, early life with me.

My mom was a brave woman, except when it came to worms, which she despised with a passion! I often wondered why she hated worms so much until she told me about her work in the tobacco plantations picking live worms from tobacco leaves with her bare fingers. For this unpleasant childhood labor, she was paid a few cents per full cupful of worms! The sight and feel of hundreds of squirming green worms was extremely unpleasant and scary to her—an experience that impacted her for the rest of her life!

When she met my dad, my mom lived with her uncle Catalino and his wife. Tío Catalino, as we called him, had returned after working on the U.S. mainland for many years. He moved to San Lorenzo and settled in an old farmhouse across the *Rio Grande de Loiza* (Loiza Large River). There wasn't a bridge, so people had to wade across the shallow part of the river to reach his house. Tío Catalino always dressed well and talked in a low monotone. When visiting others, he would sit down, talk for a few minutes, drink a cup of coffee, then depart. He was a stern man, and his face showed very little emotion. In all the visits he made to our house over the years, I never saw him smile once.

To make some extra money, Tío Catalino's wife sold hot coffee, with milk and sugar, to the workers in the sugar cane plantations in the vicinity of their home. It was up to my mom, a sixteen-year-old woman, to deliver a large metal can with hot coffee and cups to the workers during their short breaks. Many years later, my mom would tell me how uncomfortable she felt walking alone, between rows of tall sugar cane plants, under the gaze of so many adult men. She said she never complained about having to do this chore, as well as other domestic work, because Tío Catalino and his wife had given her a home. They treated her much better than other members of her family she had stayed with. As she would often tell me, "Son, I was born to work and serve others."

A few days after my dad met my mom, he decided to meet Tío Catalino and his wife to ask for their permission to visit her. To make a good impression, he wore his best clothes and purchased a stalk of ripe bananas, along with a local white cheese called *queso de la tierra*, to take as presents. At the riverbank, he took off his shoes and socks and crossed the river. He waited for his feet to dry before carrying the bananas and cheese to Tío Catalino's house.

Tío Catalino met him with an icy stare. He shook my dad's hand, his handshake conveying confidence and strength. After a few seconds, which seemed like an eternity, he invited my dad in. My mom was summoned from an adjacent bedroom to sit between her uncle and aunt.

"Señor Lozada," Tío Catalino said, "I know why you are visiting us today. However, before you say anything, I want you to follow me outside."

My dad stood up and quickly followed him. On his way out the door, Tío Catalino grabbed a machete, which he always kept by the door. My dad walked in silence, too afraid to utter a single word. Only the wind, swirling around the sugar cane plants, broke the crunching sound of their footsteps. They walked two miles to a deserted spot with a tree stump.

After my dad sat down on the stump, Tío Catalino said, "My wife and I know that you want to visit my niece and see her more often, right? Let me tell you the rules. You can visit her in our home on Sundays from one to two o'clock in the afternoon. During these visits, either my wife or I will be in the room." Then Tío Catalino turned around and returned home.

On October 9, 1941, after a few months of supervised visits, my mom and dad married. Not being able to purchase or rent a home, they moved in with my grandparents. Their house on Colón Street had multiple small living quarters in the back, with the church located in front. It was an old timber-framed house with a corrugated tin roof, which did very little to reflect the blistering tropical sun. The house did not have a bathroom, only an outhouse positioned away from the house to minimize odor and maintain privacy. It was in this house that my brothers Juan Manuel (the oldest) and Elías Abner (the youngest) and I were born.

My mom cared for my brothers and me and did household chores for my grandparents, including making special meals for my diabetic grandmother. My dad worked as an *almuercero,* or lunch deliveryman, distributing meals to the laborers in the sugar cane fields.

Those were difficult times. Puerto Rico was an impoverished island with high unemployment, poverty, and malnutrition.

11

Tropical-borne illnesses and diseases often ravaged its inhabitants. Sanitary facilities, preventive care, and state-of-the-art health clinics and hospitals were not always available. Many low-income families migrated to the mainland because they could not find work.

CHURCH

As a young wife, my mom did not have access to prenatal care. My brothers and I were delivered at home with the help of a local midwife. After my parents moved into my grandparents' home, my mom joined my grandmother's church. Going to church was a natural part of my early upbringing. It helped me develop a foundation for moral values and a sense of belonging to a community.

I was an active member of the children's group, reciting from the Scriptures and singing. These activities helped me overcome my fear of speaking in public. Some of my closest friends believed that I was predestined to become a preacher, but that distinction belongs to my youngest brother, who followed in my grandmother's footsteps.

Image 2. My dad, Juan Lozada, wearing one of his favorite outfits

Caserío de Hato Grande

When I was two years old, my dad applied for an apartment in our town's public housing project. The housing project, known as *Caserío de Hato Grande*, was one of the earliest public housing projects built under the Puerto Rican Housing Authority (PRHA). The *Caserío* included numerous one- and two-story reinforced concrete buildings, the largest ones having eight two-bedroom apartments.

Image 3. Caserío de Hato Grande (Hato Grande Housing Project).
Photo source: Housing Progress in Puerto Rico, 1938–1948
(Public Housing Administration Library)

A couple of months after applying, the *Caserío's* administrator approved my dad's application. A few days later, transporting our few personal belongings and items of furniture my parents had accumulated, we moved to an upstairs apartment in building number 10. The apartment was small, approximately 800 square feet, but to us it felt like a mansion! My brothers and I were small children, so we managed quite well. The apartment had a small balcony on the back, a private bathroom, and a shower. At my grandmother's house, our family had only had a small bedroom and the use of a communal kitchen that had to be shared with other families. Now we had an entire apartment, although small, to ourselves. My mom was ecstatic! The rental contract, signed by my dad in 1946, stipulated a rent of $3.50 a month.

When I was four years old, the Housing Authority planned to build an annex to our housing project. It would include duplex homes with gardens. My mom urged my dad to apply for one. She loved gardening, and moving to a house with its own garden would be a dream come true.

I was five years old when we moved into our new home with front and back yards. I was very excited by the move; my brothers and I now had plenty of space to play. I was also happy to see my mom so pleased with her new home. It was fun to play different games in our own yard and watch my parents plant ornamental plants and fruit trees. A few months later, the fragrant blossoms of a gardenia bush my mom had planted perfumed our summer evenings.

Our duplex neighbors were Don Francisco Rodríguez and his wife Doña Carmen. They had five children who became like sisters and brothers to me. Their house was as small as ours and they always planted the local yams that Don Francisco loved.

Our other neighbors, Don Félix López and his wife Doña Mercedes, had two daughters, Miriam and Mercedita. They were devout Baptists whose nephew became the pastor of the Baptist church for many years.

Image 4. The author and his brother, Juan M. Lozada

Together with the neighborhood kids, my brothers and I made our toys with things we found in our surroundings. I made sugar-cane-hauling trucks with small pieces of discarded wood, adding small bundles of twigs to simulate sugar cane. To complement them, I made cranes with splinters, thin cords, and small metal hooks to lift the bundles of twigs and place them on the truck beds. I even made wheels from empty Vienna sausage cans.

Playing marbles was an art. We collected marbles of many colors, invented different games, and traded them amongst our friends. These games required imagination as well as manual dexterity.

We also loved kite flying. Like the trucks, we made them ourselves with hollow sugar canes, thin sheets of paper, and glue made from flour and water. The months of February and March were the windiest and best months to fly kites. Up in the air, the kites wrestled against the wind while the bright tropical sunlight filtered through them.

Most of our childhood games were played outdoors with little or no parental supervision. Entertaining myself and learning to build toys increased my independence and confidence at an early age. It also increased my curiosity about the world and taught me how to confront challenges, work well with others, and solve problems independently. I never complained about being bored or having nothing to do—I was always busy.

Hurricane Santa Clara

The excitement generated by tropical storms always intrigued me. As soon as hurricane season began, our town was transformed by a flurry of preparatory activities. It was common to hear older adults comparing past hurricanes and reminiscing about which ones had created the most damage. To prepare each time, my dad would tape a map to the wall and listen to the weather forecasts to track the storms.

In those days, there was an organization called the *Defensa Civil* (the Civil Defense) to assist people in the event of a natural disaster or war. Volunteers were issued a khaki uniform and a hard hat. For several years, there was a curfew in San Lorenzo. At exactly 9 p.m., a loud siren would sound, and everyone except members of the Civil Defense had to be inside their homes. Anyone caught outside was taken to the police station. My dad had joined the Civil Defense and could remain outside our home longer, giving him additional time to prepare during emergencies.

In August 1956, when I was twelve years old, Hurricane Santa Clara (Betsy) hit Puerto Rico. When the weather forecaster announced that Betsy was approaching, everyone began preparations. They frantically purchased shelf-stable food, oil lamps, candles, and lumber to secure windows and doors. I remember the woodpecker-like sounds of our neighbors' hammers as they boarded up their homes. I also remember my parents filling every empty container they could find with fresh water.

Soon after the meteorologist's final warning, the sky turned dark. As the hurricane got closer, the storm clouds gathered, the horizon got even darker, and the winds howled and swirled around our house. For several hours, the winds increased and roared while we nervously waited in our living room, afraid to look outside. The rains continued—falling so hard that we couldn't see out the windows. Trees bent over, with branches breaking off and some falling over streets and roads. This was my first storm, and the forces of nature were new to me. I was in awe of the deafening sounds of thunder and the flashes of lightning.

Suddenly, the winds abated, the rain diminished, and the skies cleared as the eye of the hurricane crossed near the island. I felt relieved that calm had been restored. I was also eager to go outside and see what had happened. The calm did not last long though. Soon, the winds increased, with gusts whipping everything in sight. The sound was even louder than before! After approximately six hours, the winds and rain finally subsided. A serene calm enveloped us. My dad opened the windows and doors.

What I saw made my heart sink!

Most of our fruit trees were uprooted. I opened the refrigerator and noticed that there was no electricity; my mom reported that we didn't have water either. I walked to the poor neighborhood near the river and many of the houses were gone, swallowed by the currents of the rising river! Hundreds of trees had fallen like matchsticks, blocking the road to Caguas, and our river flooded several streets.

The old bridge to access the Florida and Cerro Gordo rural communities was blocked by fallen trees and debris. Some of my friends lived in these communities and could not access our town. This narrow bridge (the longest existing concrete slab bridge and one of the first built in Puerto Rico) was built in 1918. It was designed to be a submersible structure across the upstream course of Puerto Rico's largest river.[1]

After this horrific experience, I was very respectful of storms.

Image 5. The Old Bridge (Puente de La Marina) in San Lorenzo, Puerto Rico. Photo source: Historic American Engineering Record (Library of Congress)

THE GREAT OUTDOORS

There were no indoor sports facilities when I grew up. We played baseball, volleyball, and basketball under the hot tropical sun until dusk set behind the low tropical gray clouds. We used bamboo poles as bats and sometimes made our own baseballs. A small vacant lot behind our house became the neighborhood's favorite baseball field—we marked the bases with large pieces of cardboard held down by stones.

I learned invaluable lessons from my participation in sports: the importance of teamwork, the value of hard work, and the benefits of discipline, goal setting, and time management. Playing outdoors toughened me up and made me more resilient. Being a volleyball referee at sixteen years of age boosted my confidence and improved my leadership skills.

There were few social outlets for young people when I grew up. Our public square, built in the town's center and across from the Catholic church, was the focal point of social interaction for young people. On Friday evenings, young men sat on concrete benches or stood under the round topiary laurel trees while young women walked around in circles. Quick glances, smiles, and short phrases were exchanged, and relationships germinated. Long-term relationships as well as close friendships were initiated in this manner.

In the 1960s, the municipal government installed a TV in the public square, which increased the number of folks visiting it at night. Once or twice a week, one of my best friends (Agustín Rivera) and I walked to *La Sirena* bakery after attending Baptist church services, purchased a half loaf of freshly baked bread with butter, and sat on one of its benches to eat and talk until late at night.

There were many meaningful activities that fully occupied my time growing up. I have always felt that I had a wonderful childhood, devoid of some of the modern complications and challenges of today.

AGONY!

In the 1950s, most citizens of Puerto Rico didn't have access to well-equipped and well-managed healthcare facilities. During my childhood, medical facilities in San Lorenzo were limited. With only one physician in town, my brothers and I never saw a pediatrician. I once asked my mom how she raised us without the advice of a doctor. She said, "I used my basic animal instincts. I did what made sense to me."

There was only one dentist in our town and his primary job was to extract teeth. He practiced in the public hospital, not far away from our home. The only equipment in his meager dental room was an old barbershop chair, a few old syringes, and a set of dental forceps. He did not have a receptionist or dental assistant. Dental records were not kept, and prescriptions for medications were not given.

Very early in the morning, patients lined up under the scorching sun or tropical rain and patiently waited to have the anesthetic administered. After receiving it, they waited until all the other patients had received theirs. When they arrived at the front of the line, they could hear pulled teeth hitting a trash can inside the room and the dentist yelling, "Next!"

Patients would sit on the chair, open their mouths, and point at the hurting tooth. After a quick look, the dentist would extract it. They were given a piece of cotton and asked to press it against the bleeding spot. Immediately thereafter, they exited the room, holding a hand to one of their cheeks. The entire process would normally take fewer than five agonizing minutes!

I had two teeth pulled in this manner.

EDUCATING THE ISLAND

My parents lacked formal education, but they were fast learners. My dad had a seventh-grade education but was an avid reader and knew math and English well. He was always well-informed because he read every single page of the local newspapers. During his youth, he had the opportunity to have a personal tutor, but he quit school early, and his parents did not force him to continue. Nevertheless, he was a great conversationalist with a superb sense of humor.

Image 6. The author and his mom, Clotilde Pereira

When I was a teenager, the Education Department established an island-wide adult education program. My mom registered so she could learn to read her Bible and write her children's names. I accompanied her to school, sitting quietly as her teacher taught. Six months after her classes began, my mom had learned to read and write! As she'd achieved her goal, she quickly ended her scholastic pursuits.

My mom taught me all aspects of keeping house at an early age to help me become fully independent. "I am teaching you to do all these things in case you marry a lazy woman!" she would often tell me. The housekeeping lessons she taught me served me well, especially during my military career. Among her many lessons, I remember cooking, doing laundry, and ironing clothes as the chores that I carried with me as I grew up. I also remember the aroma of the starch my mom made from scratch for me to press clothes with.

A LIFELONG LESSON

During the sugar cane harvesting season, one of the most important chores for my brothers and me was to take a hot lunch to my grandfather, Papá Juan. My mom prepared his lunch, which usually consisted of white rice, codfish salad, one boiled egg, and a small bottle of milk.

Taking his lunch was not easy. In the morning, my dad would tell me which farm Papá Juan was working on and how to get there, but it was up to me to find him. My mother would pack the hot meal in small metal containers known as *fiambreras* (small metal bowls that could be stacked one on top of the other). The *fiambreras* kept the food warm.

Sometimes, I had to walk to their work site; other times, I would catch a bus to a spot near the workers. The fare was five cents one way. From a distance, I could see the lilliputian workers busily cutting sugar cane with their sharp, glistening machetes;

the canes falling like matchsticks. During their sparse breaks, they sharpened their machetes with a file they carried, or took a sip of lukewarm water or coffee. It was backbreaking work for very little pay.

Few sugar cane workers ate a healthy lunch. Some of them pulled a piece of dried codfish and bread from a brown bag they carried. Instead of drinking milk, they scooped water from the nearest stream with a large elephant ear leaf. I derived enormous satisfaction watching Papá Juan eat a nice meal in such terrible working conditions.

One day, my dad accompanied me to deliver Papá Juan's lunch. "Do you know why these men work in such horrible conditions?" he asked. "They work in these fields because none of them acquired a good education." My dad's statement impacted me greatly. Then and there I decided to focus on pursuing the highest level of education possible!

CHAPTER 3

BECOMING A LEADER

SOME CLAIM THAT LEADERS ARE MADE; OTHERS BELIEVE THEY are born. I believe that I was born to lead.

My leadership development began in the Pentecostal church. At six years old, my mom encouraged me to become active in the children's group. When our pastor asked for someone to recite from the Scriptures, my mom would say, "Jacob, recite Psalm 23." Despite my shyness and stutter, I never dared disappoint my mom, so I did it.

In the 1950s, many people in Puerto Rico suffered from intestinal parasites. To fight the spread of this disease, children received preventive treatment before attending school. The treatment, known as *purgantes,* consisted of ingesting two medicinal capsules of a nauseating medicine called *pasote* (made from a medicinal herb, *epazote,* known for its potency to combat intestinal worms) and a glass of clear liquid (*salsosa* or tasteless salt).

A couple of weeks after my sixth birthday, I was scheduled to start first grade at the José Cordovés Berríos Elementary School. Early that morning, my dad bought a large orange and a peppermint candy. He peeled the orange, then put it inside a cloth bag my mom had stitched for me to carry my school snacks. Next, he gave me specific instructions. "Swallow the capsules quickly with the salsosa and immediately squeeze orange juice into your mouth. After you finish, suck on the peppermint candy to diminish the lingering bad taste."

When we arrived at school, many kids wailed in anticipation of the medicine. Some pleaded with their parents to take them back home. Others would not open their mouths and were scolded by their parents. I didn't dare embarrass my dad, so when my turn came, I followed his instructions. Neither the orange juice nor the peppermint candy made the horrible taste of the capsules and salsosa any better. Belching them during the next twenty-four hours was worse!

My leadership skills continued to develop as early as my first year in school. On my first day, my dad and I went to the principal's office and learned that I was assigned to Mrs. Milagros Flores' classroom. He took me there, where I met several of my classmates. I asked Mrs. Flores if I could sit on one of the chairs. Looking at me tenderly, she said, "Of course. That's what my classroom chairs are for." Mrs. Flores' words embarrassed me, and I instantly blushed from my shyness.

I loved first grade! Mrs. Flores was a very patient and loving teacher. I made new friends and learned how to read, write, and do basic math. Seeing my progress in these basic skills made me proud and gave me self-reliance. Mrs. Flores assigned me specific tasks and appointed me to small leadership roles such as assisting her while taking attendance and helping other students. On one school report she wrote, "Jacob is a nice and responsible boy. He is very cooperative. He is doing good work." I was delighted when my dad, beaming with pride, read the report to me. For a six-year-old, those words meant a lot. I still treasure the diploma she awarded me when I finished first grade.

I attended grades seven to nine (known as intermediate school) at an annex behind the Antonio R. Barceló school. One of my favorite classes there was called *Artes Industriales*. Mr. José Luis Hernández Corretjer, affectionately nicknamed *Jim de la Selva* (Jungle Jim) because he always wore a jungle hat, taught us basic carpentry and electrical skills. His classroom was always noisy with the sound of sharpening chisels, wooden mallets hitting lumber, and the sawing of wood.

I was twelve years old when, utilizing the carpentry skills I learned, I built a bookshelf to store my schoolbooks and materials. My parents complimented me on my work and put it in our living room. This initial foray into basic carpentry formed the basis for my lifelong interest in woodworking.

We learned other skills during our *Artes Industriales* class. During the electrical skills portion, we learned how to build a small motor using batteries. We also learned to build lamps from cow horns. That was my least-favorite skill to learn. Learning these skills helped me develop creativity and problem solving— two more basic leadership skills.

DISCIPLINED

During my childhood and teenage years, most parents were strict disciplinarians, but mine were stricter than most. We had to be inside by 7 p.m. If we had not reported in by then, my dad whistled at a high pitch, and we had to run home. My parents did not shy away from corporal punishment. The lowest form of punishment was restriction of outdoor activities; the highest was a couple of well-placed swats with a belt.

One day, my dad ran into one of my seventh-grade teachers, who told him I was doing fine but had been talking too much in class. The following day, as Mr. Reyes was teaching, someone knocked on the door. When he opened it, my dad was standing outside! "I am sorry to interrupt, but may I say a few words to the class?"

The room went silent—I sat, petrified, worried about what my dad would say.

After Mr. Reyes ushered him inside, my dad stood in front of my classmates and asked me to come forward. When I stood in front, he said, "I am here because Jacob wants to apologize to you for disrupting the class." He nudged my back, and with my head bowed I said, "Mr. Reyes, I apologize for talking during class." My dad thanked Mr. Reyes and quickly stepped out of the classroom. That was the last time I disrupted a class with my conversation.

I never resented my parents' strict discipline. The way they reared me and the values they instilled in me contributed to making me the person I am today. Their strictness made me more resilient and self-controlled. The values I learned from them and the orderly environment in which I was reared were key to my leadership development.

LEADING OTHERS

I never missed an opportunity to assume leadership positions, especially in cultural and athletic activities. When our teachers sought volunteers, I was always the first one to raise my hand. I volunteered to join our school's folkloric dance group, helped my social studies teacher plan a field trip to San Juan, and volunteered to tutor a classmate who needed help with his schoolwork.

In ninth grade, I assumed my first formal leadership role when my teachers selected me to lead the class as president. When they announced my selection, I said very little, not knowing what the job entailed. My classmates did not complain about my selection—they were relieved to not have to serve as president themselves.

After being selected, I learned that I had to help plan our intermediate-school commencement ceremony and after-graduation celebration. I also had to represent my fellow students before the school authorities and act as master of ceremonies during the graduation. Flustered by the scope of my responsibilities, I immediately sought the help of my teachers and some of my closest friends. My mom, upon learning of my new job and my concerns, simply said, "Don't stress—being class president is a tough job, but you are tougher!"

Preparing for our graduation involved a considerable amount of work. I had to plan our fund-raising activities and motivate students to actively participate. I also had to prepare my graduation speech and assist our teachers in organizing my classmates during our graduation rehearsals. Although overwhelming, I was excited about the work.

I was on top of the world on graduation day! I wore the prescribed clothes, which were black slacks, a white shirt with long sleeves, black bow tie, and black shoes. After kissing my mom goodbye, I left for the town's theater. When I arrived, most of my classmates, their parents, and some of our teachers had already assembled.

Image 7. The author and his dad on his graduation day

My dad, always the first one to arrive, was there as well.

After everyone was seated and my classmates were lined up, the classical music started. I took a deep breath to calm my nerves and led the students into the theater. As we entered, the theater was buzzing with anticipation.

My dad sat on an aisle seat, clapping and pointing in my direction. I am sure he was telling all those around him that I, the class president, was his son.

Image 8. The author delivering his graduation speech

Because our school didn't have the financial resources to host a student prom, our teachers organized a graduation luncheon at the Lions Club. In those days, the club was restricted to the most affluent citizens of our town. My parents were not members, so having the opportunity to step into the club was exciting for a fifteen-year-old.

I learned more valuable leadership skills during my intermediate school years, such as how to delegate tasks and inspire others toward a common goal. I also learned to communicate more effectively and motivate others. My participation in school activities influenced my early leadership development. It gave me confidence, improved my communication skills, and helped unlock my potential.

Soon after graduation, I began my studies at the Luis Muñoz Rivera High School. Located on Luis Muñoz Rivera Street, across from a large tobacco warehouse and beside the fire station, it took me ten minutes to walk to school. At noon, I had plenty of time to go home, eat lunch, and return.

The school had approximately fifteen classrooms without air-conditioning. It lacked shaded outdoor areas, athletic fields, and a well-stocked library. We had to imagine our science experiments because we didn't have laboratories. To study advanced subjects, we had to travel to the Gautier Benítez High School in Caguas during the summer break.

During my sophomore year, I contracted dengue fever. Dengue is spread by mosquitoes and produces high fever and joint pain. There were many cases of dengue in my town. My parents emptied rainwater containers in our yard to reduce the growth and spread of mosquitoes. In addition, the local government sprayed neighborhoods with vehicle-mounted fumigating machines in the evenings. The throbbing and aching pain prevented me from going to school for two weeks.

At the end of my sophomore year, I registered to take physics in Caguas. Everything went well until I contracted mumps. Swelling of the salivary glands is the main symptom of mumps, so my mom smeared a black tarry cream (Ichthyol) on my neck twice a day to decrease the swelling. My face and neck were not a pleasant sight! Mumps prevented me from going to school, so I sent a note to the teacher requesting to take our final exam at home. Because I was one of his best students, he sent it to me. The teacher's kindness served as a good lesson to me—that, as a leader, one must make allowances for special circumstances and take care of those one is entrusted to lead.

ANTS IN OUR PANTS!

During the fall months, I oversaw the design and building of the stage for our church's Christmas play each year. Our pastor, knowing I had the required leadership abilities, put me in charge of the project. In addition, I could draw and paint. With limited resources, we made do with whatever we could find.

One Christmas, we built a stage with a narrow trail leading to a manger. I suggested live plants to make the scene more realistic. Since we couldn't purchase them, we gathered clumps of dirt with weeds from the countryside, transported them to the church, and placed them by the trail. On the day of the play, excited parishioners filled our small church. In the last scene, shepherds and the three wise men arrived at the manger and knelt before baby Jesus. Everything went well until one of the shepherds knelt by one of the clumps. He jumped up and yelled, "Ants, I am being bitten by ants!"

I closed the curtain and ran to the stage, only to see hundreds of ants crawling all over the floor! We had inadvertently brought in an anthill. To this day, my youngest brother, who was one of the shepherds, and I laugh our hearts out when we remember that play! I learned an important lesson from this funny episode: not to leave things to chance. To avoid potential risks, one must plan meticulously.

Communication

When I was fifteen, I left the Pentecostal church and joined the Baptist church because it had a very active youth group. In addition, it presented me with more opportunities to lead and grow as a leader. Being in a leadership position was important to me for a couple of reasons. First, I had developed the ability to motivate others. Second, as a youth leader, I could make a stronger contribution to the church.

Upon joining, the pastor immediately asked me to teach Sunday Bible school. Subsequently, I led church services, preached, and served as treasurer. These activities further enhanced my self-confidence and public speaking skills.

Draw What You See

Around my sixteenth birthday, the municipal government of Caguas offered free art classes on Saturdays. I enjoyed drawing, so I registered. The trip to Caguas (in large buses without air-conditioning) covered seven miles, took approximately forty minutes, and cost ten cents for the round trip. The buses were worn-out and not well maintained—their floors sounding like they were caving in.

The art instructor was Mr. Víctor Torres Lizardi, an accomplished local artist who grew up in a family with limited financial resources. He was a man of few words. A childhood injury had stunted his growth, so he stood at only five feet tall.

During the first class, I expected him to explain which charcoal pencils or paper to use, but he placed a white marble bust of a young girl on top of a table and said, "Draw what you see." Drawing the bust was difficult, but doing it under his intense gaze was almost impossible. I could not figure out how to begin because I focused too much on its shape and color. I touched the cool marble several times to get a better feel for its shape. After anxiously trying to draw the bust without success, I was about to give up.

When Mr. Lizardi noticed my difficulties, he said, "You are trying to draw the way the bust is. That is not the key. Try drawing the bust the way it looks, not the way it is." I told him I didn't understand what he meant. "Imagine a forest," he said. "We know that leaves are green, but when you look at them from a distance, they don't all look green, right? Some look green, brown, or even blue. It all depends—among other things—on how the light strikes them and their position. Instead of drawing the bust the way it is, why don't you draw what you see?"

I looked at the bust again and saw different colors, shades, and light variations. An hour later, I completed my first art lesson. I was thrilled!

We learned both oils and charcoal in that class, but I preferred charcoal—it was a more docile and gentler medium. Mr. Lizardi used the art lessons to teach me that things are not always what they seem. We may think that life is one way, and it turns out to be something quite different. To this day, I have that first drawing in my office.

During my junior year of high school, I tried track and field. I quickly realized I lacked the skills for those events, so I turned my attention to chess. San Lorenzo had some very good chess players, and I learned to play while sitting on the benches of the public square. Fernandito Martínez (who subsequently became the chess champion of Puerto Rico) and Carlos Buitrago (a schoolteacher) taught the rest of us how to play this beautiful game. On Saturdays, engulfed by the clicking sound of chess pieces hitting the chessboard, we would play all day until nightfall.

I became an avid chess player, studying its many strategies and following international tournaments. The intense immersion required during chess matches helped improve my concentration at school and in other areas of life. Chess taught me the value of strategizing, thinking ahead, and patience. Seizing unexpected opportunities and evaluating all options before choosing one were also important. Those lessons not only helped me win many rounds of chess; they also gave me the tools to succeed in my future professional careers.

Early in the year, I was elected president of my senior class. This time, the election was by the direct vote of my classmates. Although the position required more work and responsibility than my ninth-grade graduation, it presented another opportunity to enhance my leadership skills by working with my peers, coordinating events, and giving more public addresses.

My senior year was a busy year for me. Besides my duties as class president, I also continued with my church leadership activities. At school, I became a member of a scholastic team that competed against other high schools on a TV program called *El Club 6* (The Six Club). These timed competitions required extensive preparation and practice. My assigned areas were world geography and history. Our teachers, classmates, and parents had their eyes glued to their television sets when our team competed—the pressure to do well was intense!

In preparation for college, I visited the University of Puerto Rico (UPR) in Río Piedras several times to acquaint myself with the campus and its surroundings, including the ROTC building. I was interested in the ROTC because graduates received a commission to serve as officers in the military. I also met with our school counselor often to learn about scholarships and work study program opportunities at the UPR.

Two weeks prior to graduation, my dad purchased my graduation shoes at the Thom McAn store in Caguas. Buying clothing with my dad was always an experience. He would take me to *Casa Palacios*, owned by Mr. José Palacios Ramírez, where he purchased on credit. He always selected my clothes and bargained for the price. It didn't matter if he was buying oranges, bananas, or clothing, my dad *always* bargained for a better price! I loved watching my dad negotiate, so I watched and learned his techniques for getting a better deal. To this day, I often find myself applying his skills when I travel to countries where bartering is customary and figuring out the point at which the other person is willing to yield and quickly make an offer.

Back then, I used these skills to help my classmates acquire new suits for our prom and graduation. As the class president, I knew that many of my classmates wanted to look good, but they lacked the finances, and this was my way of helping them. One Saturday morning, I traveled to a clothing store in San Juan to talk to its manager. I explained that I was the president of my high school class, and I needed his help. I told him I could convince many of my classmates to purchase their suits from his store if he gave us a discount. He was so impressed that I had traveled so far that he promised to send a salesman to our high school and give us an escalating discount based on the number of suits purchased. As I exited the store, the adrenaline rush made my body shake with excitement.

A week later, a salesman showed up at our school with several suits. Within two weeks, twenty-five of my classmates had signed up, we were promised a 20 percent discount, and everyone was happy! Three weeks later, I went to pick up my suit. When I went to pay for it, the cashier told me there was no charge. They had sold so many suits that, in appreciation, the store manager wanted mine to be complimentary. As class president, my idea was a total success. I also felt a tremendous sense of accomplishment in helping my classmates.

Afraid of what others might think, I would not accept the suit until I discussed it with our class advisor. My goal was to help my classmates, not to benefit myself with a free suit. She said there was nothing wrong with me accepting a free suit as I had not asked for it—it was a gift from the store. The following Saturday, I brought home my first suit! Before I left Puerto Rico, I gave the suit to my dad and, for many years, he wore it for special occasions. Sixty years later, that gray suit is still in my bedroom closet as it carries a unique and special meaning.

A Father's Pride

I had written my commencement speech with the help of my teachers, emphasizing the students' appreciation of them and our parents. I also added some words to motivate my classmates to keep learning, stay focused, and not limit themselves by circumstances or obstacles in life. I spent hours rehearsing the speech to make sure it sounded right. Still, I was so nervous on commencement day that my mom made me a lemon blossom tea to calm my nerves. The tea was wonderfully fragrant, tasting like the smell of lemon flowers. It also had a slightly bitter note. After drinking it, I felt more relaxed and my nerves were at ease.

I put on my graduation cap and gown and checked the graduation speech I had prepared before walking to the town's theater, located in the public square. As I walked, neighbors stepped onto their balconies to wave and congratulate me, filling me with a deep sense of accomplishment and pride.

The town's movie theater, *Teatro Cervantes*, accommodated about 300 people. The stage was narrow, and the chairs had wooden seats and black metal frames. Black-and-white movies, mostly filmed in Mexico, were shown on weekends. Outside the theater, the students congregated on the sidewalk, where two teachers lined them up by height. I led the students inside to Giuseppe Verdi's triumphal march "Aida," the anthem of choice for high school graduations in Puerto Rico. As I walked by my dad, who was seated along the theater's main aisle, I heard him say, "That's my son, Jacob!"

Seeing my dad clapping and mentioning to everyone sitting near him that I was his son, was very emotional. I've always believed that every son wants his dad to be proud of him. At that moment, my dad expressed his pride publicly and for everyone to hear.

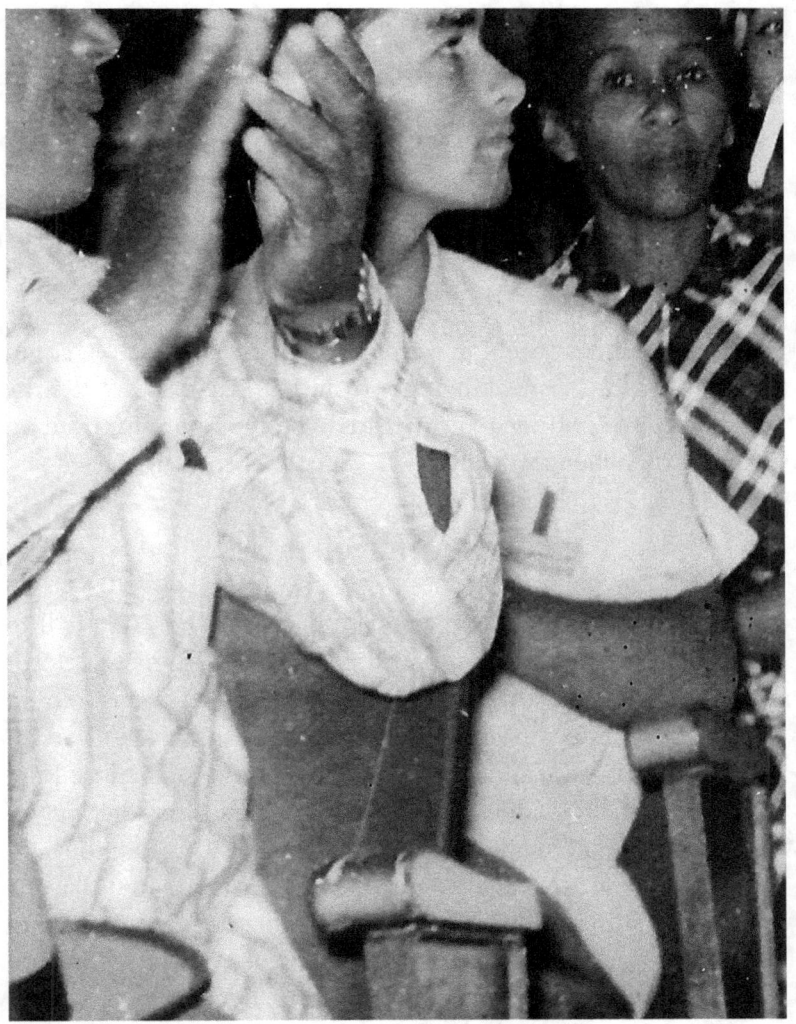

Image 9. The author's dad, Juan Lozada, clapping during his high school graduation

When the last of my classmates sat down, I walked to the front of the stage. After thanking our parents and teachers for their love and encouragement, I asked the students to rise and sing our class song before I delivered my speech. I had spent hours at home rehearsing the speech, memorizing most of it, and ensuring that it sounded right. The time spent preparing, and my mom's tea, had worked. My nerves had calmed down and the delivery was flawless.

After the principal spoke, we lined up to receive our diplomas. When my turn came, he also pinned a gold medal on my chest for obtaining the second-highest grade point average in our class.

I was proud of myself for facing my fears of public speaking, but at the same time I reflected on areas in which I could improve for future speaking opportunities. I didn't want to miss any chance to continue to grow and do better before I moved on to my next challenge: college.

LEAVING HOME

After our graduation, I began to prepare for the UPR in Río Piedras. I had chosen to attend the UPR because it was closer to home, it had a strong ROTC program, and it sponsored an extensive calendar of cultural activities. The university had an excellent chess club, and the campus was also near the José Raúl Capablanca Chess Club in San Juan, named after the Cuban chess prodigy and former world champion. Visiting that top club would enable me to learn from some of the island's best players. I had invested considerable time and effort to learn chess and yearned to learn more and improve my game. Visiting those two chess clubs would allow me to achieve these goals.

When I applied to the UPR, I learned that a new student enrollment policy required students from the eastern part of the island—including my hometown—to enroll, for their first two years, at the recently established Humacao Regional College instead of attending Río Piedras. Students would be transferred to Río Piedras at the end of their second year. The new campus was an experiment to bring higher education closer to the people. I was heartbroken about this change; I felt that my efforts had been frustrated.

Humacao didn't have a strong ROTC program, nor did it have proximity to the chess club in San Juan, museums, or a student center. The UPR was everyone's top choice and aspiration; Humacao, on the other hand, was a new and unproven educational experiment. For several days, it was difficult for me to concentrate. Though I wasn't excited about the change, the college awarded me a full-tuition scholarship plus $50 a month for room and board. My dad's uncle Deco, a self-taught landscaper, lived behind Humacao Regional College. He agreed to let me live with him.

I had mixed emotions about moving to Humacao. I had never stayed away from home and knew I was going to miss it and my parents—especially my mom's cooking. On the other hand, college life was an opportunity to make new friends, discover new horizons, and learn more about myself. It would help me figure out what I wanted out of life and explore potential career paths. Going to Humacao was not the outcome I'd wanted, but I had to make the best of it, even if it was begrudgingly.

Prior to leaving, my mom helped me pack my clothes in a small suitcase. I asked and received my parents' blessing (asking and receiving our parents' blessing is a longtime tradition practiced in Puerto Rico). After several hugs and admonishments, I left to catch the bus to Humacao. Leaving my parents' home and thinking of what college life might bring sent shivers down my spine.

The bus stop was located near the telegraph office on the street parallel to the elementary school, where I had entered Mrs. Flores' classroom twelve years earlier. After I sat on the bus, I glanced across the schoolyard to her classroom and saw the spot where, many years earlier, my classmates and I had assembled to take the awful medicine to kill parasites. Some of my classmates and other passengers filed into the old bus, and soon the driver started the vehicle. As always, there was no air-conditioning. We

41

made a right turn and, after making a couple of stops to pick up other passengers, left town.

Buses seldom traveled at speeds exceeding 25 miles per hour, and passengers could embark and disembark at any point during the journey. Humacao was 15 miles from San Lorenzo, but sometimes it took two hours to get there. It was a long trip, but it was a beautiful ride along twisty rural roads lined with fruit-laden guava and mango trees.

Two hours later, the bus arrived at the public square, known for its huge and beautiful ficus trees pruned in ball-shaped topiaries. The trees had been planted by Tío (Uncle) Deco decades before.

Image 10. The author's children, Valerie and Jason, with Tío Deco in front of one of the trees he planted

Arriving at the public square brought back many memories. For many years, Tío Deco would sit every afternoon on his favorite bench in the public square to admire the beautiful and majestic trees he had planted. These beautiful giants—which he called his "beloved children"—became a lasting testament to his artistry and love for the city of Humacao and its people.

Eight of my high school classmates were on the bus. Like me, they were excited about starting their college life but disappointed that they had to attend the Humacao Regional College. As soon as we disembarked, with our small suitcases and bags in hand, we said our goodbyes and dispersed ourselves around the city to our respective boardinghouses.

The following morning, I registered for classes. The deafening sound of hammers and the smell of fresh paint emanated from the incomplete classrooms. The college was established in a large classroom building and a group of old mansions with ornate facades, wood siding, and wrap-around porches in downtown Humacao. The library, administration offices, cafeteria, and laboratories were established in the old mansions. The ROTC drills were conducted outdoors.

My high GPA put me in advanced classes, in competition against students from private high schools. I had attended a small public high school that lacked many resources. However, the standards had to be applied equally to all students, so I understood that I had to work harder than others to succeed. The Humacao campus offered ROTC, as well as fencing, and I decided to enroll in both. There were good reasons for choosing fencing. Besides its physical fitness benefits, fencing would improve my decision-making, discipline, self-confidence, and the ability to react quickly under pressure.

From Disappointment to Opportunity

The ROTC instructor was Lieutenant Colonel José Escribano, a heroic Army infantry officer who spoke perfect English and was one of the highest-decorated Puerto Rican Soldiers during the Korean War. He was also from San Lorenzo. Learning that our ROTC instructor was from my hometown made me proud. Lieutenant Colonel Escribano's exemplary military service served as a motivator and an example for me to emulate.

The fencing instructor was Professor Jean Lesieux, a Frenchman who—according to local lore—had been exiled to Brazil by the French government. Professor Lesieux possessed uncanny reflexes and incredible speed for his age. Like a fox, he could react rapidly, change direction, and swiftly lunge forward. In the two years that he taught us, none of us came close to scoring a point against him.

I enjoyed fencing. Professor Lesieux made fencing fun, competitive, and tough. We competed against each other three times a week; we finished exhausted and drenched with perspiration. After six months of instruction, Humacao Regional College excelled at fencing. One of our fencers, Zaida Casals (now a retired teacher), distinguished herself by defeating the reigning female champion of the UPR in Río Piedras during a tournament held in San Juan. With very little training, she beat a fencer with much more experience and coaching. Her performance inspired me and exemplified how one could conquer challenges and triumph against a formidable opponent.

Though initially disappointing, Humacao Regional College soon turned into an opportunity to further my education and leadership skills. I carried a heavy academic load. It included Introduction to Mathematics, Study of the Western Culture, Basic Course in English, Introduction to the Physical Sciences, Basic Course in Spanish, Social Sciences, ROTC, and College Algebra and Trigonometry.

I also organized a chess club and led a small group of chess players in local tournaments. With my classmate José M. García Leduc, I ushered the effort to designate the owl as the school's mascot. These opportunities began to tamper my disappointment about the regional college. My new thoughts were that, despite its shortcomings, the Humacao experiment was going to benefit me and my classmates.

ROTC also enhanced my leadership skills. During my first year, I was accepted into the National Society of Pershing Rifles, a military-oriented honor society for college-level students. It was considered the nation's premier undergraduate leadership development organization. I had to learn how to lead cadets during physical training exercises, parades, and drills. I also had to motivate other cadets during everyday situations and training exercises. To motivate others, I challenged them, set clear goals and expectations, and praised their accomplishments. I also set an example.

I was also a member of the ROTC drill team, a highly visible part of the ROTC program and our college. With its fancy steps and rhythmic cadence, it gave exhibitions during ROTC parades, events held at the college, and events in the city of Humacao. Being part of this team was a source of great pride to me.

While fencing improved my physical fitness, ROTC improved my proficiency in English as their instruction was conducted in English, and we were expected to communicate in this language during our drills. To motivate us to speak English, our instructors added "demerits" to our academic record if we spoke Spanish during our drills.

Because I was able to influence others and was dependable, I became one of the informal leaders of the student body. Students respected my ability to build relationships between them and the faculty and identify opportunities on their behalf.

COLLEGE REPRESENTATION

There were four major universities in Puerto Rico, and they all competed in track and field annually at *Las Justas Intercolegiales* (The Intercollegiate Games). The schools' athletic directors organized the games, and one student leader represented each campus team.

Owing to my demonstrated leadership abilities, our athletic director chose me to represent our college, so I accompanied him to an organizational meeting in San Juan. Our athletic department was not fully organized, so we could not compete in the games. However, we were invited to attend the meeting and the games as observers. Attendees included athletic directors of the various campuses. Others were renowned athletes whose names I'd seen in the newspapers. I was in awe at being in their company. During the meeting, the athletic directors discussed the schedule of athletic events, logistical arrangements, and pre-game activities.

Upon my return to Humacao, I shared the results with some of my classmates and floated the idea of organizing a group to attend the games and represent our college. They liked the idea but felt that we should obtain permission from the chancellor to be absent from class during the games. None of my friends felt comfortable doing it, so I volunteered. The following morning, I visited the chancellor's office and shared the idea. He agreed enthusiastically! He asked me about my extracurricular activities. When I told him that I had organized a chess club, he said he enjoyed playing too. After that encounter, I visited his office several times to play chess. I believe that my willingness to do what other students wouldn't opened this door for me.

The universities participating in the games had their own songs, but our campus did not have one. I discussed the problem with some of my friends, but we couldn't agree on a song because there were too many ideas and opinions. After a lengthy discussion—and lacking a consensus—I returned to Tío Deco's house, sat on the balcony, and began to brainstorm ideas. The chords of "La Marseillaise" rang inside my head. As I started to write, my ideas turned into a short song:

> Viva nuestra alma mater,
> viva el Colegio Regional.
> Lucharemos por el bien, el amor, la libertad,
> amaremos el saber, el valor, y la verdad.
> Llevaremos cuan pendón la bandera del honor
> del Colegio Regional.
> Viva nuestra Alma Mater,
> viva el Colegio Regional.

Translated:
> Long live our Alma Mater,
> long live the Regional College.
> We will fight for the good, love, freedom,
> we will love knowledge, courage, and truth.
> We will carry as a banner the flag of honor
> of the Regional College.
> Long live our Alma Mater,
> long live the Regional College.

After our college approved the use of our song, we sang it loudly as we traveled in public school buses to the games being held in San Juan.

EVENTS AND RETREATS

I continued my involvement in the Baptist church youth group and was elected president of the Central Youth District. We organized events at different churches, and religious retreats at a conference center in the mountain town of Cayey. I helped plan the retreats with our youth counselors Ms. Petra Urbina and Ms. Irma Violeta Cruz. My responsibilities included helping look for venues for our retreats, making suggestions for each retreat's program, and marketing the retreats among our youth. Though I'd never organized events like that before, my past experiences as class president gave me the confidence I needed for these new tasks.

On one occasion, we invited a well-known quartet to sing at a retreat. Much to our disappointment, they could not attend. Not wanting to disappoint the attendees, I gathered three of my best friends—Neftalí Rivera, his brother Rubén, and Carlos Álamo—and suggested we create a quartet. Rubén, who had an angelic voice, took the lead and asked that I sing bass. Neftalí and Carlos sang tenor and baritone.

For our first rehearsal, we assembled under the shade of a large tree and sang the first stanza of the spiritual "I Shall Not Be Moved." The result surprised us—our voices harmonized beautifully! After we sang the spiritual several times, we added a couple more. We practiced the three hymns for a period of one hour to make sure we were ready. Taking the initiative to organize the quartet was an unexpected leadership opportunity. To witness how well we harmonized gave me a sense of accomplishment and satisfaction.

After our successful debut at the retreat, we met on Saturday afternoons for six months to rehearse and learn new hymns. We had been good friends before the quartet was formed, but the rehearsals strengthened our friendship. Our love and attachment to each other grew. Our reputation also grew, and we received invitations to sing in other churches. I was astonished by our sudden notoriety because we had only been practicing for less than a year.

COMPLETE AND OVERCOME

At Humacao, ROTC occupied a considerable amount of my time. ROTC is a nationwide college program that prepares students to become officers in the military. Students take military courses, get leadership training, and receive scholarships. It is a regular college class that can count as elective credits toward a student's degree.

Our ROTC program had two phases: the Basic Course and the Advanced Course. The Basic phase was conducted in Humacao and the Advanced phase was in Río Piedras. Each phase was two years long. Advancing to the second phase was very competitive—it was based on scholastic achievement, demonstrated leadership, and formal interviews with our instructors. My track record in these areas became instrumental in my selection. Near the end of my second year, I was selected to attend the Advanced phase. I was ecstatic! It validated my leadership abilities and made me feel very proud.

Moving to Río Piedras to continue our studies was not easy. I left behind the comforts of a private room at Tío Deco's home and had to move into a boardinghouse with twenty other students. Approximately 267 students attended the Humacao campus. Río Piedras had approximately 26,000. The Humacao campus was small—it covered three blocks. The Río Piedras campus was enormous—it extended over 200 acres. I felt lost, out of place, and lonely. It took me a couple of months to fully adjust to the new environment and feel comfortable in my new surroundings.

In Río Piedras, ROTC cadets were assigned different roles and responsibilities by our senior instructors. I was responsible for the Corps of Cadets newspaper (collecting articles, taking photos, and editing the paper). In addition, I coordinated the participation of the Army National Guard band and invited guests to our monthly parades.

One benefit of joining ROTC was the opportunity to be commissioned as an Army officer after graduating from college.

My goal was to earn a commission and serve in the military to enhance my leadership skills, earn financial security, and travel. I planned to serve for only two years, return to Puerto Rico afterward to study law using the GI Bill, and rejoin my church activities.

To be commissioned, one also had to successfully complete a mandatory summer camp at Fort Bragg, North Carolina. To prepare us for summer camp, our ROTC instructors held a two-week pre-summer camp at Camp Santiago, an arid, desolate, and hot military installation in the southern part of Puerto Rico. Then in June 1966, about twenty-five ROTC cadets traveled from Puerto Rico to Fort Bragg in a cold, noisy, and cramped military aircraft. We sat on side benches, with little cushioning, facing each other. This was my first trip to the mainland, and I was excited. I was also nervous because we had little information about the camp. We didn't have a program of activities and didn't know what to expect. Soon, we would find out.

Summer camp was a grueling two-month training program in which we were treated like Army recruits. Days were long and training intense. We were awakened at 5 a.m. by a sergeant screaming and hitting a garbage can with a heavy stick. Fifteen minutes later, we had to run outside to do one hour of physical training. We traveled on dusty roads to receive tactical training out in the open, fire our assigned weapons, and learn military maneuvers. We were not allowed to walk anywhere—we had to run. Lights out (the time to be in bed) was 10 p.m. and was strictly enforced. Our days were long!

Leadership roles rotated daily among cadets. You could be assigned to lead a squad (ten cadets), a platoon (three squads would be thirty cadets), or a company (three platoons would be ninety cadets). When your time came, you had to be ready to perform. Unfortunately, my turn came during an exhausting three-day field training exercise. I had to lead my platoon of thirty cadets through various tactical situations under simulated combat conditions.

On one occasion, I directed my platoon to dig foxholes to protect ourselves from simulated enemy fire. We slept in the foxholes all night, taking turns to guard our positions. The constant noise, fear of the unknown, and lack of sleep added to our stress. We had been well trained, so I was confident and on autopilot during the exercise. Despite the tension and challenges, evaluators complimented my organizational skills and calmness under stress.

At the end of the physically and mentally challenging two-month camp, I had successfully completed all requirements and overcome all obstacles. The return flight to Puerto Rico was short in comparison. We were all excited to go back home and spent the time in the military aircraft playing dominoes and sharing camp stories.

As an Advanced Camp ROTC student, I had a contractual obligation to join the Army right after graduation. That would require a move from Puerto Rico to the mainland, so I decided to move home during my senior year to spend more time with my parents before leaving the island. To cover my travel expenses, I got a part-time job in the university's library that paid fifty cents an hour, and I worked forty hours a month. Added to a thirty-seven-dollar monthly stipend I received from being an advanced ROTC student, I made enough money to cover my monthly travel expenses.

Moving home was a bad decision though. ROTC drills were held on Tuesdays and Thursdays at 3 p.m., ending at 5 p.m. I took public transportation to and from San Lorenzo and never got home before 9 p.m. On regular class days, I walked several blocks from the university to the Rio Piedras public square, caught a bus to Caguas, and transferred to another bus to my hometown. Sometimes, I arrived too late to catch the last bus home and walked several blocks to the road leading to San Lorenzo in hopes of hitching a ride.

I spent an average of six hours a day commuting. I was always worn out when I arrived home. As soon as I walked through the door, I would collapse on the sofa. My mom would reheat dinner while I took a quick shower. Before long, it would be time to go to bed and start all over again.

Because I would be joining the Army, I had to list three military career choices a month before my graduation. From these, the Army would select which one I was to follow. I listed Medical Service Corps (my first choice), Army Intelligence (second), and Artillery (third).

I chose Medical Service Corps because it would open doors to jobs in the healthcare field. I also felt that my science background would be more in tune with service in Army healthcare. After weeks of anxious waiting, I was given my first choice. I also received written instructions to report to Fort Sam Houston, Texas, to attend the Basic Officer Leader Course to learn the basic leadership skills required of an Army officer. I was very happy about my assignment. Texas sounded like a good place to begin the next chapter of my life as a Soldier.

When graduation day arrived on July 9, 1966, I proudly wore my Army uniform during the ceremony. The years of hard work, dedication, and sacrifice had been worthwhile. Equally important, the many sacrifices my parents had made on my behalf had finally paid off. I was the first member of my family to graduate from college and the first to receive an Army commission. I was very excited and thankful for the many blessings bestowed upon me but also nervous about what the future might bring.

CHAPTER 4

JOINING THE U.S. ARMY

I WAS COMMISSIONED AS A SECOND LIEUTENANT IN THE U.S. Army a couple of hours before my graduation ceremony on July 9, 1966. Senior Army officials, my ROTC instructors, and relatives—including my parents and one brother—joined me. As it was customary for relatives to pin the shiny gold bars on the cadet's uniform, my mom, my dad, and I rehearsed at home the day before the ceremony. My dad was particularly impressed by the ceremony. He loved America and always impressed upon me the fundamental values of our nation: freedom, equality, and justice. Having a son commissioned in the U.S. Army was a source of great pride to him.

During the ceremony, I could not stop thinking about the sacrifices my parents had made—my dad landscaping yards during weekends so I could have extra spending money and my mom laundering, starching, and pressing my ROTC khaki uniforms so I would look my best. I remembered my parents' efforts to provide me with a safe, disciplined, and loving home environment, my dad's frequent visits to school to check my grades, and their unyielding support when I was class leader.

Seven days later, I left my hometown for the San Juan International Airport. I still remember my mom standing by a window facing the street as I placed my suitcase in the car that would take me to the airport. As I departed, I looked back and noticed that her eyes were misty, and her face showed considerable sadness. As a young man, I didn't understand the pain in saying goodbye to a departing son or daughter. It wasn't until I had children of my own that I understood that feeling.

Image 11. The author's parents, Juan Lozada and Clotilde Pereira, pinning his second lieutenant bars

At the airport, I met five other young Puerto Ricans who had received their Army commissions and were traveling to San Antonio. Three of them were Army nurses and two, like me, were Medical Service Corps (MSC) officers. Although my traveling companions were strangers, I was comforted by the fact that they were also going to Fort Sam Houston to attend the same Basic Officer Leader Course. After a twelve-hour delay, we arrived in Texas, exhausted, to oppressive heat that pressed into the airplane when the doors opened.

At Fort Sam Houston Headquarters, we reported to the officer on duty, and he directed us to the Bachelor Officer Quarters (BOQ), located four blocks away. We grabbed our suitcases and scurried away, hoping to find a comfortable bed at the other end. Two of my traveling companions—Ángel Luis Olivieri and José "Tato" Miranda—shared a three-bedroom, un-air-conditioned apartment with me. The third one, Víctor Valdés, was assigned his own one-bedroom apartment. The apartments were sparsely furnished; they contained just the basics—beds, sofas, and kitchen tables. Two large fans moved the air around, but they did little to mitigate the oppressive summer heat.

The following day, a Sunday, my friends and I woke up hungry. Not knowing where to go, we walked aimlessly, hoping to find a place to eat. We walked past green manicured lawns, historic buildings, and the Officers' Club. As we approached the Calvary Baptist Church on New Braunfels Street, the pastor saw us and stepped outside to invite us to worship. Embarrassed, I said, "We appreciate your invitation, but we are four hungry Army officers who are new to this city and need a place to eat." He directed us around the corner to Earl Abel's Restaurant.

It was noon when we arrived, exhausted and starving. Every table was taken in this highly popular restaurant, a favorite among senior citizens. After a short wait, we were seated. The aroma of hot coffee and fried bacon drifted to our table, making us hungrier. We ordered the biggest breakfasts on the menu and ate until we were full. During our meal, we got to know each other better, talked about our families back in Puerto Rico, and wondered what our first day in the Basic Officer Leader Course was going to be like. It was our last meal together before immersing in our new life as Army officers.

Monday morning at 7 a.m., I started the MSC Basic Officer Leader Course, an eight-week training program that included everything from customs and traditions of the Army to tactics and employment of medical units during war. Because our nation was involved in the war in South Vietnam, our training included the history, customs, and traditions of the Vietnamese; the political background of the war; and a tour of a mockup Vietnamese village. We also learned field medicine and practiced how to employ Army helicopters for medical evacuation.

The heavy brass rhythms of a military band welcomed four hundred new officers as we assembled in the Medical Field Service School (MFSS) quadrangle between four buildings: the classrooms, administrative offices, Officers' Club, and a mess hall. The officers included physicians, nurses, medical specialists, and MSC officers. Those who, like me, had undergone ROTC training or had previous military experience were able to follow the various military commands and instructions. But for those who had been commissioned without any military training, it was a different matter. It was hilarious to see some formations of officers being given a command and half of them turning right and the other half turning left, stumbling into each other like a rack of dominoes.

After some initial instructions, we began our administrative processing by completing many forms and questionnaires requiring personal information. Two of the documents we had to complete were a will and a power of attorney, bringing into sharp focus the serious nature and potential sacrifice of our chosen military career. Next, we were taken to a basement to pick up a box of military books. Afterward, we marched to a large theater to continue our orientation.

In the afternoon, we started physical training on a grassy field across from the MFSS. A psychologist, who had no prior military experience, was assigned to lead our platoon. A soft-spoken individual, he took his job seriously. He stood in front of our formation to lecture about the dangers of the high temperatures, the need to stay hydrated, and the different types of heat injuries. I stood in the front of the formation. As he spoke, his voice turned into a whisper, his face turned pale, and his legs wobbled. Suddenly, his eyes rolled back and he slumped to the ground without saying a word. I was shocked when I saw him hit the ground like a sack of potatoes and worried that something terrible had happened to him. Three of us stepped forward to carry him to the shade and give him water from our canteens. After resting and cooling off for forty-five minutes, he recovered and rejoined our platoon. Our newly appointed leader had become the first heat casualty during our first day of physical training.

After eight weeks of lectures, daily physical training, and field training exercises, we completed our Basic Officer Leader Course. I was relieved that our training had ended and impatiently awaited my first job in the Army. Our graduation was held at the Fort Sam Houston theater. I marched into the theater with the rest of my fellow officers to the rousing tunes of an Army band. I felt tremendous pride and a sense of accomplishment as I received my diploma. I was also excited because soon I would embark on a new and stimulating adventure—my first job in the Army.

Tato and I were assigned to the U.S. Army Medical Training Center (MTC) and Ángel Luis to Brooke Army Medical Center at Fort Sam. I was very happy with my assignment because the MTC provided excellent leadership opportunities for young officers. These opportunities would make me a better officer and enhance my military record. In addition, I did not have to move from Fort Sam. I liked the Hispanic environment of San Antonio and staying at Fort Sam would make my adjustment to my new life in the military much easier.

My friends and I were no longer students, so we had to vacate the BOQ and look for an apartment. We settled on Bel Meade Apartments across the street from Fort Sam. We could walk to work, military stores, the Fort Sam Theater, and the

Officers' Club. Rent, not including utilities, was $90 a month. With a monthly military pay of $300, we could afford the three-way split.

The apartment didn't include a washer or dryer; we used a communal laundry facility in one of Bel Meade's buildings. It didn't have air-conditioning either; we relied on "water coolers" on the windows. The coolers were boxes with a fan and water inside. They didn't work as intended, but that did not inconvenience us because we never had air conditioners in Puerto Rico.

Our apartment had one bedroom, so we added a rollaway bed and used the living room sofa as a third bed. We agreed to rotate between the beds, and I prepared a roster for the sleeping rotation. Ángel Luis worked the night shift in the hospital, so our arrangement worked well—during the week, there were only two of us in the apartment at night.

I became the conscience and moral compass for my roommates. Before they left the apartment for social activities, I reminded them that they were Army officers and should behave accordingly. To me, being a commissioned officer meant more than a military rank. It meant maintaining higher standards of personal conduct and being good role models. One of the leadership principles we learned stated, "Set the example." As officers, we were expected to respect others, maintain high moral standards, and avoid any actions that could compromise our integrity.

On September 9, tingling with excitement, I traveled by bus to my first military job as training officer in Company A, Second Battalion (Alpha Two) of the MTC. I was assigned to a unit that taught Soldiers to become Army medics. My primary duties included serving as principal assistant to the executive officer of a training unit. I also had to work closely with Soldiers, supervise training, teach several classes, and act for the executive officer in his absence.

I was in high spirits when I arrived at Alpha Two. A wooden poster with the photos of the top leaders of the unit greeted me: company commander Captain Ricardo Alba and First Sergeant Walter Mazur. I thanked the good Lord for giving me a Hispanic commander. I thought he would be more patient and supportive. I reported to Captain Alba's office. His blank look and lack of expression sent cold shivers up my spine. After a brief introduction, he asked if I had any questions. Unsure how to respond, I asked, "Sir, at what time does work start in the morning?"

Without smiling or making eye contact, he said, "Lieutenant, we start physical training at 5:30 a.m., if you care to join. Any more questions?" I said no and left his office. So much for having an understanding Hispanic boss.

As I stepped out, a skinny noncommissioned officer (NCO) with a thundering voice said, "Lieutenant, welcome to Alpha Two; nice to have you on board!" The welcoming voice belonged to First Sergeant Mazur—one of the most competent NCOs at the MTC. After his warm welcome, he introduced me to other NCOs and showed me around the building. I was immediately impressed by him. He was extremely knowledgeable about Army regulations, and other NCOs treated him with great respect and deference.

After thanking him for showing me around, the First Sergeant said, "Lieutenant, I assume that you are going to join us for physical training tomorrow morning." After I said yes, he continued, "Great! I don't know if you are aware that Captain Alba was an accomplished football player in college, and he and I have an ongoing competition on who can do more push-ups. I hope you can join us!" And with a big smile, he turned around and returned to his desk. I was left standing, thinking that my first day at the U.S. Army Medical Training Center had not gone as planned. I began to worry.

One of the many qualities that distinguished First Sergeant Mazur from others was his on-the-spot corrections. One day, I was on the phone talking in Spanish with my friend Tato. Upon hearing me, the first sergeant yelled, "Lieutenant Lozada, you are in the United States Army now, speak English!" I continued my conversation in English.

During the fall, the temperatures in San Antonio dropped from the high 90s into the low 60s. For someone who had lived in the tropics all his life and hated cold weather, it was an unwanted change. One morning, I stood wearing my summer uniform, shivering outside the Charlie Two building as I watched our Soldiers march to their classrooms. Master Sergeant Birdsong, one of our most senior NCOs, asked if I was okay. I told him I was fine, but it was too cold for me. He asked if I had a military field jacket. I did not, because I felt it was too early in the fall to purchase one.

Two hours later, he walked into our building with a military field jacket for me. I asked where he found it, and he said, "After I saw you shivering, I walked to the barracks and, suddenly, an Indian chief wearing a beautiful feather headdress stepped from behind a tree with this jacket and said, 'Birdsong, I bet you have someone in your unit who needs this; take it to him!'" I didn't know what to think about the Indian chief story. Too stunned to ask Birdsong, I walked into First Sergeant Mazur's office later and asked him about it.

"That story means never ask an NCO where he obtained something," replied First Sergeant Mazur. NCOs pride themselves in "making things happen," so as a young officer, I had to trust them.

MTC had some unique individuals. One of them was our battalion commander (Captain Alba's boss), a lieutenant colonel with a deep Texan accent who disliked junior officers. For some reason, he could not stand dead flowers and walked around checking the landscaping and the plants in front of each unit. When he found a dead flower, he would curse and get very upset. On one occasion, he verbally reprimanded a junior officer for having dead roses outside of his office. A few days later, I was walking down the sidewalk when the lieutenant colonel approached me. I saluted. "Good morning, sir!"

He looked at me in an agitated manner and said, "Lieutenant, report to my office in ten minutes." I felt on edge about this order, not knowing what he was going to do when I reported to his office. Five minutes later, I walked into his office. He walked circles around me like a raging bull while lecturing about the importance of the hand salute. He asked me to salute again. While I stood at attention, he criticized everything about my military posture. Next, he whispered, "Salute twenty times." I saluted twenty times and stopped, still standing at attention. "Is that all, sir?" I asked.

"That's all, lieutenant. You are dismissed."

I turned around and rushed out of his office. I had reason to be angry and offended, but instead, I looked for ways to improve my military salute. From this unpleasant experience, I also learned, early on in my military career, how not to treat those entrusted under me.

In contrast, two weeks later, I met Colonel Arthur Edward Britt—the executive officer of the MTC. He was trim and fit, always impeccably dressed without a wrinkle in his heavily starched uniform. He always listened intently, squinting his deep blue eyes, making one feel like the most important person around. He talked softly but with such authority that you couldn't help but be mesmerized. On one occasion, after a parade, he told us that he valued and appreciated us and the great job we were doing. He encouraged us to continue taking care of our Soldiers and balance our personal lives and our Army's responsibilities. I always wanted to emulate Colonel Britt. His leadership inspired me to always look the best in uniform, be an active listener, and take good care of my Soldiers.

DUTIES

We kept a frenetic pace in Alpha Two, working six days a week. Saturdays were dedicated to military parades, distributing the mail, tutoring Soldiers who had fallen behind, cleaning the barracks, and landscaping. Weekdays, I inspected the barracks (bunk beds and lockers) and common areas of approximately 200 Soldiers every morning at 6 a.m. I also made sure that Soldiers attended training.

As a Class A officer, I picked up payroll at the Fort Sam Finance and Accounting Office and paid each Soldier in cash at the end of the month. For this important duty, I carried a loaded .45 caliber pistol. At the Finance and Accounting Office, I received a stack of money and a statement certifying that the amount given to me was correct. The statement also said I was responsible for the money as well as any discrepancies found once I left the building. I never signed the statement without counting the money at least three times.

Image 12. The author, as Class A Officer of Alpha Company, 2nd Battalion, MTC, getting ready to pay his Soldiers

I also served as officer of the guard once a month (a job that required me to stay up all night to supervise a group of Soldiers guarding key buildings at Fort Sam), defense counselor (advising Soldiers during courts-martial), and battalion Christmas decoration officer (figuring out a theme, procuring the decorations, and supervising their setup). Christmas decoration officer was the worst job at MTC because the officer selected was the last one allowed to depart on vacation during the Christmas break. I despised this job.

There were some MTC traditions that also occupied my time. On Thanksgiving Day, officers were expected to dine with the Soldiers in the mess hall, wearing their most formal dress blues uniform. Officers' attendance was mandatory. We were also required to attend sporting events and talent shows our units participated in. Because my unit always participated in both events, my work hours extended from 5 a.m. to 9 p.m. Mondays to Fridays. As officers, we were also expected to attend happy hours on Friday evenings at the Officers' Club. These many responsibilities and important roles were mine at only twenty-two years old!

As Army officers, we were evaluated annually using an Officer Efficiency Report (OER). I worked extremely hard during the early months of my Army career and was rewarded with an excellent OER. It stated:

> Lieutenant Lozada is an exceptional young officer. He has handled his duties in a highly exceptional manner, constantly seeking to further improve the activities of this unit.
> Lieutenant Lozada has proven himself to be the type of officer who continually strives to find a solution to a problem regardless of the obstacles involved. He has worked diligently to reduce the failure rate of the trainee personnel within the unit, and at this moment, his efforts are to be highly commended due to outstanding results. He has made a tremendous contribution to the unit in

that he has continually strived to maintain standards
of excellence as far as personal appearance of trainee
personnel is concerned. He settles for nothing less than
perfection in every phase of unit training.

Lieutenant Lozada can be a tremendous asset to the
United States Army, with the capability of being an
outstanding career officer, if he so chooses to remain in
the service.[1]

On March 21, 1967, I was transferred to Company C, Second
Battalion (Charlie Two) to assume the role of executive officer.
This transfer was considered a promotion in recognition of my
excellent performance in Alpha Two. As executive officer, I became
the second officer in command of a medical training unit with 400
Soldiers. I also substituted for the commander in his absence.

Four months later, on July 9, 1967, I was promoted to first
lieutenant, which included my first pay raise and no longer having
to perform the onerous duties assigned to second lieutenants.
Wearing my heavily starched uniform, I couldn't stop smiling
during my promotion.

My new boss was an easygoing captain who had been in the
Army one year longer than me. He gave me free rein to do my
job and allowed me to supervise a second lieutenant as I saw fit.
He invited me to his home for dinner several times, giving me
ample opportunity to socialize with him and his lovely wife.

Image 13. The author's promotion to first lieutenant

IMPROVING MY ENGLISH

A few months after my transfer to Charlie Two, the captain told me that, although I was an excellent officer with great potential, I needed to improve my English. Annoyed, I told my friend Allan Miller about the conversation. He admitted that he wanted to improve his Spanish. We agreed to help each other. At work, whenever I made a mistake in English, Allan winked at me, a signal to see him in private to correct my mistake. He also introduced me to new words and phrases. To reciprocate, I stopped by Allan's house on weekends and spent a couple of hours talking to him in Spanish and correcting his pronunciation.

To further practice my English, I purchased a tape recorder, recorded myself reading articles from the daily newspapers, and played them back to hear myself. I also signed up for a training course at the MTC called "Methods of Instruction." The course developed confidence and improved speaking skills for instructors. I was the only officer enrolled in the course, but that did not concern me. At home, I watched English TV programs instead of Spanish ones. The same was true for the movies. San Antonio had a theater showing Spanish movies, but I went to the Fort Sam Theater to watch movies in English whenever possible. In three months, my English improved dramatically.

A year after we moved to the apartment, our living arrangements changed. Tato got married and moved to a house at Fort Sam. Two months later, Ángel Luis also got married and moved to an apartment in San Antonio. I now had the apartment to myself. Soon thereafter, I met a young lady from Houston and fell in love. When I met her, she was visiting her aunt, an employee of the Personnel Office at the MTC. After a six-month courtship and engagement, we got married at the Fort Sam chapel and moved into an apartment a few blocks away from Fort Sam.

Marrying an Army officer presented some challenges to my young wife. She would have to adapt to the demands of military life, navigate the frequent relocations, and endure the loneliness that would come with my extended absences due to service commitments. Despite these obstacles, she provided unwavering support during my stressful assignment at the MTC.

She quickly became familiar with the customs, traditions, and protocols of the Army. Active participation in the Officers' Wives Club helped her understand and connect to our military community. Her adaptability extended into our family life, where she helped foster an atmosphere of peace and fulfillment in our marriage.

Even though it was my job to oversee and help a second lieutenant and the NCOs in our unit, there were times when they helped me as much as I helped them. One morning at work, my company commander received a letter from a local bank complaining that one of our NCOs signed checks without having the necessary funds. I had met the NCO when I arrived at C-2 and talked to him often to discuss issues related to the Soldiers under his supervision. Angered by the letter, the commander directed me to show the NCO how to balance his checkbook. After the customary, "Yes, sir," I realized I had never had a bank account, so how could I counsel the NCO?

I visited the Fort Sam Houston National Bank to ask for help. I explained my situation to one of the tellers, and she opened an account for me. She also showed me everything about check writing and maintenance to avoid overdrafts. The following day, I shared everything I had learned with the NCO. I felt uneasy, at twenty-three years of age, counseling someone over twice my age about something so personal, but he thanked me for my help and never had another problem keeping his bank finances. I kept my bank account, and for many years thereafter, the Fort Sam Houston National Bank provided me with banking services.

A couple of days after I counseled the NCO, Lieutenant Colonel Joseph R. Territo became my battalion commander. Like General George S. Patton, he always carried a swagger stick and smoked cigars. Shortly after his arrival, he informed us that the Army Surgeon General was going to visit the MTC. He was a very important visitor, so Territo asked for ideas to impress him. I remembered how well my ROTC drill team at Humacao performed and asked for permission to organize one. He gave me the green light—as long as participating Soldiers did not miss training.

That evening, after delivering the mail to the Soldiers in front of the barracks, I asked for volunteers. I told them I wanted the sharpest-looking Soldiers in the unit, and they had to commit to practice every weekday after dinner. The following day, thirty Soldiers volunteered. I selected twenty-four, based on how good they looked in uniform. I worked with the supply section of the MTC and arranged for them to wear khaki uniforms, a maroon

67

ascot (a broad necktie the color of the Army Medical Department), and a helmet. Next, I taught them the choreographed sequences and precision steps we performed at the ROTC, as well as new ones I had learned from a drill team manual I borrowed from the Fort Sam library.

Our practices went well, and my Soldiers learned the steps quickly. I was not worried about their performance. When we demonstrated our routine to Lieutenant Colonel Territo, he was so impressed that he included the drill team in the Surgeon General's schedule. We continued practicing daily until our routines were perfect.

When the Surgeon General visited, we began our performance as soon as he stepped out of his vehicle. After we finished, I presented him with a specially designed military helmet. When he accepted it, I felt relieved and proud—my Soldiers had performed their precision moves flawlessly. "This is the first time I have seen an Army medics' drill team," he said. "This must be the only drill team in the Army Medical Department." When I heard those words, I was overwhelmed with admiration for the efforts and hard work of my Soldiers. When I told them, a loud cheer of jubilation echoed around Charlie Two.

Later that evening, as I pondered the success of our drill team, my mom's teachings came to mind. It didn't matter the task at hand, she always gave it her best. My drill team had given their best, resulting in a flawless performance. They had committed themselves to being superlative and volunteered many hours to achieve that goal.

PROMOTION?

Near the end of my two-year military commitment, an officer from the MTC personnel office called me to discuss my future. He said I was doing an excellent job and, if I extended my commitment, I would be promoted to captain with a pay increase. I told him I was not sure I wanted to pursue an Army career and was planning to return to Puerto Rico and study law. On the other hand, I had done a good job as training officer and executive officer and received excellent job performance evaluations.

The prospect of being promoted and getting a pay increase appealed to me. There was another important issue to consider: my young wife. She did not speak Spanish and knew very little about the Puerto Rican culture. Moving there would have been difficult for her. A final consideration was the war in South Vietnam, which was at its peak. By extending, I ran the risk of being sent, but that did not bother me. I had trained for war and relished the opportunity to apply what I had learned.

After much consideration, I decided to extend my military commitment. I also decided to stay in the military and reach the rank of colonel. After I made the decision, a feeling of sadness and gloom washed over me. By staying in the Army, I would not be able to see my parents often, nor return to my church activities. On July 6, 1968, at twenty-four years old, the MTC commander promoted me to captain.

A few days after my promotion, Lieutenant Colonel Territo asked to see me. I rushed to his office. With the departure of our company commander, he needed to find a replacement. Chomping on his cigar and leaning toward me, he said, "How would you like to take over Charlie Two?" It was a huge undertaking to lead ten older NCOs and be responsible for approximately 260 Soldiers, but I was elated by the offer. It was a testament to my performance and Lieutenant Colonel Territo's confidence in my abilities. Excitedly, I said, "Thank you, sir, for having such confidence in me. I accept the job."

He then looked at me intently and said, "Be aware that it is going to be 'do or die.' If you don't do a good job, this could be the end of your military career."

To make the job easier for me, he offered me any one thing that would help me. Without hesitation, I said, "I want Master

Sergeant Candelario as my first sergeant." Master Sergeant Candelario was a key member of Lieutenant Colonel Territo's staff. He was also from Puerto Rico and had served in the 65th Infantry Regiment during the Korean War. He knew practically everyone at Fort Sam, was easygoing and persuasive, and had a great reputation among officers and senior NCOs. Lieutenant Colonel Territo turned red, closed his eyes, and cursed himself for making the offer. After his anger subsided, he told me I could have Candelario the following day.

LEARNING ON THE JOB

Every morning, a long line of Soldiers anxiously waited by my office. They had, during the previous day, committed an offense (been late for training, missed bed check, or slept in class). As their commander, I administered administrative punishment (restriction to the barracks, extra duties, or fines) depending on the offense. When First Sergeant Candelario first noticed the line of Soldiers waiting to see me, he proposed an alternative to my process: he would handle the small offenses first, then refer repeat offenders to me. His idea made sense, so I gave him permission to take over.

The following morning, I overheard First Sergeant Candelario as he handled one of the Soldiers in trouble. He inquired as to what had happened, and after the Soldier—trembling with fear—confessed his offense, he said, "Son, do you understand that what you did was wrong?" After the Soldier replied in the affirmative, he continued, "Now that you understand that, you owe me two weeks of grass cutting." Next, he warned the Soldier that if he repeated the offense or committed a more serious offense, he would refer him to me for more serious punishment. He finished the counseling session by opening a green notebook and recording the Soldier's name, offense, punishment, and date.

Image 14. The author in front of Charlie Company, 2nd Battalion, U.S. Army Medical Training Center, a unit recognized for the academic achievements of its Soldiers

He repeated the same conversation with the rest of the Soldiers, always ending with, "You owe me one week of pulling weeds" or "You owe me one week of painting the inside of the barracks," and so on. A few weeks after First Sergeant Candelario's arrival, we had the best-looking outdoor and indoor areas in the entire MTC with freshly painted barracks, new signage, and well-maintained landscaping with grass neatly trimmed and free-flowering rosebushes. I also saved hours a week on discipline. By handling those minor infractions, Candelario freed up my time for more important tasks like counseling Soldiers, building relationships with other MTC commanders, and providing guidance to my NCOs.

First Sergeant Candelario was a blessing for other reasons. Sometimes, when he noticed I was quiet and under a lot of stress, he would call his Puerto Rican wife and ask her to cook lunch for "his Captain." Then he would invite me over. As we walked to his home, he asked how things were going and gave me fatherly advice. Over a mouthwatering plate of rice, beans, and stewed chicken, we would converse about our families in Puerto Rico and other issues unrelated to the Army. The aroma of tropical spices and Puerto Rican food reminded me of my home on the island. For a young officer like me, those lunches were relaxing breaks from a stressful environment.

The continuous competition among units was one of the key stressors at MTC. Units were graded in several ways: the appearance of their outdoor areas, the number of disciplinary actions administered to the Soldiers, the number of Soldiers who passed exams, and participation in sports and talent shows. Units achieving the highest scores were recognized publicly during officers' monthly meetings. Recognitions such as this one were important; they played a key role in our annual efficiency reports.

My unit excelled in three of the four areas; however, my Soldiers struggled with academics. Trying to learn the root cause of the problem, I asked for individual test results and noticed many of our Hispanic Soldiers had failed their written exams. I talked to some of them and discovered they didn't fully understand the complicated medical terms taught in English. After discussing the problem with First Sergeant Candelario, I established an evening tutoring program for Hispanic Soldiers who needed additional help. I enlisted him, a Mexican American NCO, and bilingual Hispanic Soldiers to become tutors. I also volunteered. Instantly, my Hispanic Soldiers' academic performance improved, and our overall academic scores soared. Within a couple of weeks, our unit had the fewest disciplinary problems and highest academic performance in the entire battalion!

BUILDING FRIENDSHIPS

I learned the value of relationship building early on in my career. One day, I noticed a nicely dressed lady leaving an office building. I introduced myself and was surprised when she said, "I have heard about you from my husband Joe—Lieutenant Colonel Territo!" My conversation became more formal because I wanted to make a good impression. As we continued talking, she asked if I spoke Spanish. I said yes and told her about life in Puerto Rico and Texas. She listened intently, with a warm smile and inquisitive eyes. She'd moved to the U.S. from Spain. After our initial encounter, we had many conversations in Spanish.

After she told me about her husband's love of strong coffee, I prepared some Puerto Rican coffee and took it to him at work. The lieutenant colonel loved it! After that initial taste, I purchased an electric coffee maker for my office, and we had a cup every morning. I learned much about Territo and the Army from those early cups of coffee. I also learned that developing trust and connection with others could be an invaluable asset as I progressed through the Army ranks. It would foster a sense of belonging and help me adapt better to Army life.

One day, we were informed that Colonel Britt was being reassigned. Though I didn't work directly under him, I was disappointed by the news because he had been a role model for the young officers at MTC. Colonel Britt's replacement, Colonel Jack D. "Blackjack" Wallace, was the opposite. Everyone feared his explosive temper and impatient demands.

One day, I parked my car in a space adjacent to Colonel Wallace's space. As I entered the building, Colonel Wallace walked by me in a hurry to leave. A few seconds later, he returned and exploded like a grenade. "Someone is parked in my reserved parking slot! Who is he?" I knew it wasn't me, so I remained in my seat.

A couple of minutes later, a captain walked in. "Do you own a blue and white Chevelle Malibu?" he whispered. I did. "Colonel Wallace wants to see you outside."

I rushed to the parking lot. Colonel Wallace pointed at my car. "You are parked in my reserved parking space!" he angrily yelled.

I clearly was not. The rear tire of my car barely touched the white line dividing the parking slots. Alarmed, yet deferring to his rank, I replied, "I am sorry, sir. I won't park in your space again." I was annoyed at Colonel Wallace but kept my emotions under control. He was the second-highest ranking officer at the MTC and deserved my full respect.

When I returned to my office, First Sergeant Candelario shared some bad news—he had been reassigned to Fort Lee, Virginia. The news troubled me. We had developed a great leadership team; he had become my right hand, a good friend, and trusted advisor. I was saddened but understood that the needs of the Army always come first. I had a long and emotional conversation with Candelario prior to his departure. I thanked him for all he had done for me, Charlie Two, and my Soldiers. I also wished him well in his new job. At the end of the conversation, I could hardly restrain my emotions; it was difficult for me to say goodbye.

First Sergeant Wayne Bishop replaced First Sergeant Candelario. I didn't know what to think of Bishop when he walked into my unit carrying a Bible under his arm, smoking a cigarette, and talking in a booming voice. "I read the Bible every morning before the start of my workday," he said. "I hope it doesn't bother you." I was taken aback by Bishop's statement. He was obviously someone who wasn't intimidated by rank and spoke his mind freely.

I responded, "It doesn't bother me at all, First Sergeant."

A chain-smoker with a quick temper, rumor had it that an altercation with an officer in South Vietnam cost Bishop a promotion and resulted in being transferred to the MTC for his last military assignment. A practical nurse, he excelled at diagnosing and treating basic medical problems. Few of our Soldiers were able to trick him into sending them to the barracks with a fake illness. After Bishop arrived, our sick call rates dropped dramatically, improving the number of our Soldiers attending training. And the more Soldiers who attended training, the better our performance as a unit.

Image 15. First Sergeant Wayne Bishop, Charlie Company, 2ⁿᵈ Battalion U.S. Army Medical Training Center, top Non-Commissioned Officer

More troubling news arrived when Lieutenant Colonel Territo announced his departure. Losing such a great leader was difficult to accept. I loved his leadership style and had developed a strong professional relationship with him. Prior to his departure, he surprised me with a letter of commendation, which included:

> You have shown that you are a superb commander. You have been especially effective in improving the morale and esprit of the members of Company C and contributing greatly to the effectiveness of their Republic of Vietnam training. Congratulations on these outstanding feats on your first try as unit commander. I wish you continued success and look forward to a military association in the future.[2]

I was touched. Saying that he looked forward to a military association with me in the future was a great compliment for a young officer. Commendation letters, such as this one, were important to an officer's career as they were placed in the officer's personnel file to be considered by promotion selection boards.

Major Pine replaced Territo, arriving from South Vietnam. He had never led Soldiers and was sloppy—his shirt was always bunched around his waist and his boots were never polished. He did not carry himself as a military officer. Like Bishop, the major was sent to the MTC for his final assignment. I could tell that First Sergeant Bishop did not like him. Neither did I, but he was our boss and deserved our respect and loyalty. One morning, the major informed me that he was coming to visit Charlie Two to inspect our barracks. I informed First Sergeant Bishop, and he immediately picked up the keys to open the doors.

The major arrived and, narrowing his eyes, immediately started to make suggestions. I advised him that Colonel Pixley— the MTC commander and our boss—liked things a certain way, but after being strongly rebuked, I kept my mouth shut. In one latrine, he angrily stated that he didn't like the cream color on the walls. I tried to convince him that it was the only color the Fort Sam engineers had, but he would not budge. Finally, First Sergeant Bishop, with that scorching look in his deep blue eyes, said, "Major, Captain Lozada has told you that the engineers only had that color, so what is it that you don't understand?"

The major looked down on him. "I don't care what color of paint they have. I am ordering you to repaint this latrine!"

I knew about the first sergeant's temper, so I quickly got in between them and led the major outside to avoid escalation.

Two weeks later, Colonel Pixley visited my unit. He was a physician with a great reputation as a meticulous and highly effective leader. When he complimented us about our low sick call rates and the scholastic achievements of our Soldiers, Bishop and I looked at each other and smiled proudly. Then he mentioned that he wanted to see the barracks. As he spoke, the major joined us. First Sergeant Bishop led us into the barrack the major had toured. When he walked into the latrine, freshly painted in a pitch-black color, Colonel Pixley recoiled in horror. "Whose idea was it to paint the walls black?"

First Sergeant Bishop, without skipping a beat, said, "Sir, I painted the walls cream, but the major ordered me to repaint them with whatever color the Fort Sam engineers had. They only had black paint—I followed the major's orders."

"That's the stupidest idea I have ever heard! First Sergeant, get some cream paint and repaint this awful-looking latrine. And Captain Lozada, you know how we do things at MTC, don't let this happen again!"

"Yes, sir," I loudly replied.

Colonel Pixley stormed out of the barrack, leaving the major with his mouth wide open. After this incident, the major never again bothered us with his suggestions.

I learned an important lesson from this incident. As a newly arrived leader, it is tempting to exercise one's authority and direct immediate changes. A better approach is to spend time learning about the organization and its environment first. After that incident, I always took time to learn about the unit I was assigned to before ordering changes.

Changes

I was approaching my second year at MTC when my career management officer called. Without much explanation, he told me that I was being transferred to Fort Hood, Texas, 150 miles north of Fort Sam. I had to report to Fort Hood on August 5, 1968. The news floored me; I didn't know what to say.

My next job was operations officer and headquarters detachment commander of the 36th Medical Battalion. As the operations officer, I was going to be responsible for planning and coordinating operations, training, and logistics for the battalion. As detachment commander, I would be responsible for managing various aspects of security operations (including security inspections and enforcing safeguards for classified material), logistics, and human resources of the headquarters staff. I was ambivalent about this assignment. The job was challenging; it provided opportunities for growth because it involved areas with which I was unfamiliar. However, I wasn't looking forward to moving my family to Fort Hood.

It was customary to pay a courtesy visit to the MTC commander prior to an officer's departure, so I made an appointment to see Colonel Pixley. He knew the purpose of my visit and complimented my work, even informing me that he'd called the Pentagon, asking to keep me. I was deeply moved by his words; they were a testament to my job performance at the MTC.

When I arrived at Fort Hood, I drove to the 36th Medical Battalion and was met by a bevy of activity all around. I walked into the headquarters building, asked to see the battalion commander, and was shown to his office. The battalion commander was Lieutenant Colonel Loren Fryar.

When I entered his office, I noticed several cookbooks on his desk instead of Army regulations, military pamphlets, or manuals. I subsequently learned that he was an amateur chef. I stood rigidly at attention in front of his desk and saluted. He introduced himself and said, "Captain Lozada, I know that you come from the MTC, where everyone cuts their hair short and does physical training daily. In this unit, we don't worry much about those things. We have other priorities."

I told him that I wanted to learn more about my job. He looked at me and, with a big smile, said, "Captain, I can only tell you that you are assigned to this unit. The rest is confidential." Then he picked up a copy of a *Newsweek* magazine that he had on his desk. "I am sorry I can't tell you more at this time, but if you read this magazine, you might learn a few things." The magazine featured an article on Russia's invasion of Czechoslovakia. The U.S. was sending an armored brigade from Fort Hood to Germany with combat support units as a show of force. Lieutenant Colonel Fryar didn't have to say anything else—it was obvious that the 36th Medical Battalion was going to Germany, and I was going too! I was dumbfounded by the unexpected news. I wished my career management officer had mentioned to me that my next job involved a deployment overseas.

In my new job as operations officer, I was responsible for the pre-deployment training and transportation of troops and equipment to Germany. My assistant, Master Sergeant Borcherding, was twice my age and experienced in military operations. After he explained a draft deployment plan he had prepared, he asked about my deployment experience. Admitting that I had none, he said, "We can do things based on my experience or we can do things based on yours. Your choice." I wanted to learn as much as possible from him, so I leaned on his experience and recommendations.

The stress of preparing for deployment and the long days we spent training in the vast bivouac areas of Fort Hood clobbered me, and I became ill the day before leaving for Germany. The following day, I boarded a C-141 Starlifter Air Force aircraft with a high fever and sore throat. The noise and cold temperature inside the aircraft made my symptoms worse. Maintaining a normal conversation was difficult, and we had to wear ear protection during takeoffs and landings when the noise was even louder. I was shivering throughout the flight and my body ached.

I felt uneasy about leaving my young wife alone in our modest rental house near Fort Hood. The thought of her being by herself while I was away weighed heavily on my mind. To address my worries, she chose to stay with her parents in Houston. This decision brought me reassurance, knowing she would be safe and comfortable in the company of her family.

Our trip to Germany took over fifteen hours, and we arrived at Ramstein Air Base during a snowstorm. It was the first time I had seen snow. It looked beautiful—a white blanket covering rooftops, trees, and sidewalks. Cold air filled my lungs while I blew on my hands to keep them warm. Unfortunately, the beauty of it was short-lived.

The following day, despite my illness and the weather, we began a 400-kilometers long convoy of military vehicles to a training area in Grafenwoehr, Germany. I rode in an Army jeep with a small heater and little protection against the cold and blustery winds. Although we had winter parkas and heavily insulated boots, my hands and feet were cold as ice and my nose was numb.

The convoy included more than thirty vehicles that struggled to maintain control in the snow and ice. Despite our training, we could not avoid accidents or drivers getting lost. It was my job to organize the convoy and keep the vehicles together, so—with a map in hand and a radio in my vehicle—I communicated with all drivers, paying particular attention to any vehicle that fell out of the convoy. It was dark when we arrived, hungry and exhausted. We set up our operations center in an old, grey concrete building adjacent to a mess hall before going to our barracks for a well-deserved shower and rest.

A couple of hours after we went to bed, an officer woke me up, shouting because something was crawling over his body. He removed his shirt, and I noticed lice crawling over his skin. I removed my shirt and was appalled to notice the same! I was disgusted by the lice and immediately called for transportation to take us to the hospital. Three hours later, we returned with delousing cream and the hope of a couple of hours of sleep. This was my first overseas deployment, and I was sick, cold, and covered with lice. I couldn't help but feel frustrated.

Our deployment also included training in support of combat operations. I worked closely with Lieutenant Colonel Fryar to solve the tactical scenarios and military exercises we faced in Germany. He had served in Germany before and knew the country very well. He also had extensive knowledge about the employment of medical units. We both had offices in an old building heated with coal-fired furnaces.

Once, I received a message from headquarters asking about a particular scenario. I took it to Lieutenant Colonel Fryar's office and, after reviewing it, he casually said, "Jake, the Army Field Manual FM 31-8 states that we should do such and such, but I think that the correct answer is as follows: 'Maintain our units in their current position and see what else develops.' What do you think?" After I provided my input and we agreed on the final answer, I sent it to our headquarters. Their officers always tried to stump us with the most difficult and tricky tactical problems, but we gave them the correct answer every time!

My first deployment taught me a lot about the differences between domestic and foreign training. Though our long hours of training at Fort Hood had sometimes felt monotonous and unnecessary, they were key to helping us adjust quickly to a new environment, which allowed us to perform well under stress.

After two months in Germany, we returned to Fort Hood, but military housing was not available there, and the nearby city of Killeen didn't have many rental homes available. This shortage forced me to rent a 1,000-square-foot duplex, so small that when my wife and I had friends for dinner, one of us had to sit on the bed in front of the dining table because there wasn't enough room for everyone. Despite the cramped space, my wife and I adjusted to our new home. We purchased some items of furniture, and she decorated the house. I made some needed repairs to make it more comfortable for us. Life at Fort Hood was good, but Soldiers don't train to remain in their military installations in the U.S. They train for war.

It was 1969, the height of the Vietnam War, and I wanted to apply what I had learned to a combat zone. My friends Tato and Ángel Luis were already in South Vietnam, and I felt I should go too. Although I had been at Fort Hood less than a year, I called my career management officer and volunteered. He thanked me for volunteering but said he had a different job for me in South Korea as executive officer of the 618th Medical Clearing Company. I was extremely disappointed about not going to South Vietnam but had no other choice but to accept the job.

The Army would not allow my young wife to accompany me to Korea. However, I could return home for a short vacation six months into my tour—at my own expense. Prior to my leaving, we purchased a home in San Antonio. I was worried about leaving my wife by herself, but I was comforted to learn that during my absence, she would also spend some time at her parents' home in Houston.

KOREA

I arrived at the Kimpo International Airport in Seoul three weeks later, after a long and exhausting 17 hours of flying, with stops in Seattle and Alaska. On the drive to Camp Nabors, I was astounded by the sheer number of old buses, cars, and military vehicles competing for space on the road against old men and women pulling carts loaded with vegetables and fruits. The acrid smell of diesel fuel and the heavy dust from factories irritated my lungs and made my eyes itch.

Upon arrival at Camp Nabors, I reported to the installation commander before being escorted to the 618th Medical Clearing Company. The 618th managed several health clinics in different locations on the peninsula. Because the unit provided healthcare, the commander was a physician, even though he had been drafted into the Army and had very little military training.

As executive officer, I performed all administrative duties of the clearing company. Additional duties included ensuring that our field equipment was well maintained, training Soldiers in chemical and biological warfare, managing the property of the unit, supporting the orphanage, and securing classified documents. In addition, I managed the recreational facilities at Camp Nabors and paid the Soldiers.

Image 16. The author with Doctor Stephen Rando at the Camp Nabors Dispensary

As the orphanage officer, I collected funds from our soldiers to purchase rice, milk, and clothing for a Korean orphanage, which Camp Nabors supported. Once a month, I also took excess milk from our dining facilities to the orphans. Seeing the adorable faces of the children—and the orphanage staff bowing deeply to show their gratitude—filled me with a sense of accomplishment and gratitude for the opportunity to make a small contribution to the children's lives. I often wonder how many of these precious orphans grew into adulthood, attended school, and became contributing members of society because of our efforts to help them.

On one occasion, I brought the orphans to Camp Nabors for a special meal with our Soldiers. I felt that it was important for the Soldiers to see the children they had been supporting with their monthly donations. Our Soldiers mostly interacted with Korean soldiers. Holding the precious children, eating with them, and talking to the orphanage staff helped them see a different face of Korea and its people. The Soldiers teased the children throughout dinner, eliciting giggles from them and bursts of laughter from the staff. Everyone was smiling when they left the mess hall.

AN ADDITIONAL ROLE

A couple of months after my arrival, I was called to the commander's office at Camp Nabors to talk about the Officers' Club. The colonel wanted to hear a newcomer's perspective about why members didn't patronize it. From what I'd heard in my conversations with others, most officers felt that Friday happy hours did not provide enough value for the dues they would have to pay. They also felt that happy hours weren't relaxing enough to entice them to go. Some also felt that the dues were unfair because the lowest-ranking officers paid the same dues as the highest-ranking officers.

I suggested changing dues to align with rank; the colonels would pay the highest amount and the second lieutenants the lowest. That would encourage more low-ranking officers to attend because they could better afford the club dues. I also suggested special Friday dinners on a bi-weekly basis to celebrate officers' arrivals, departures, and promotions. The colonel was so impressed with my suggestions that he named me the Officers' Club officer.

The new appointment overwhelmed my already full schedule. I now had to plan the Friday dinners in addition to my assigned duties. While my schedule was busy, life in Korea continued to provide new ways for me to learn about the country and its people. I visited various museums in Seoul, traveled to other military installations in the peninsula, and went to dinner often with a Korean captain who worked at Camp Nabors.

Despite my other roles, maintaining unit readiness was my most important duty. Our dispensaries provided healthcare services during peacetime, but we had to be ready to support American and South Korean forces in case of war. This dual mission was not easy to accomplish because our field equipment and vehicles required weekly maintenance. Maintaining the equipment competed against the Soldiers' time to provide healthcare, so I had to schedule maintenance sessions on weekends and holidays. Our Soldiers resented it, but our readiness mission came first.

We also had to conduct field training exercises in a wartime location several times a year in case the North Koreans invaded the South. Our assigned location was 100 miles south of Seoul, near a riverbank surrounded by rice fields. I led the unit through tortuous roads using a well-worn military map. Upon arrival, and with the help of our NCOs, I selected the areas to park our military vehicles and place the tents with our medical and communications equipment, the Soldiers' sleeping areas, and the mess hall.

After the unit was set up and organized, we familiarized our Soldiers with the unit's field medical equipment and supplies. Stored in heavy gray metal chests, they had to be inventoried and tested prior to use. We also trained our Soldiers on protection against chemical and biological agents, how to physically secure our area, and use of our communications equipment. The intense exercises lasted three to five days, but they not only kept us ready, they also provided us with a break from the monotonous life at Camp Nabors.

Maintaining communication with my wife was difficult. Our contact was restricted to once every two weeks through a military auxiliary radio system (MARS) station. This program relied on amateur radio operators, who helped service members connect with their families. To reach my wife, I would patiently wait at the station for a connection to the mainland. Once a link was established, the operator dialed her number; we had fifteen minutes to speak. These short calls demanded careful planning, making every shared moment both meaningful and difficult.

Those long-distance phone calls were filled with anticipation and excitement. Despite their brevity, our conversations were honest and heartfelt. Simply hearing my wife's voice brought immense comfort, alleviating the loneliness and anxiety that came with our separation.

MISSING FAMILY

Of all the experiences I had in Korea, I remember the bitter cold the most. On one occasion, a fellow officer invited me to go shopping in Seoul. Because of the cold and fog, I could see small ice particles in the air. I jumped and moved around to warm up as we waited for a taxi. As we rode into town, I ran my fingers down one of the frosty windows. I tried very hard to adjust to the cold Korean temperatures, but to no avail; I was always cold during the winter months.

To make matters worse, I was the assigned officer of the guard on Christmas night—I had to walk the one-and-a-half-mile perimeter and inspect the guards, dressed in heavy clothes and weapons ready, at various intervals. The temperature was approximately nineteen degrees Fahrenheit. Although I wore the required winter uniform and boots, I was frozen to the bone.

The snow made crunching and popping sounds as I walked. I thought about my family and friends back in Texas and sunny Puerto Rico on that dreary, dark, cold Christmas night. I felt like a piece of me was missing.

When I arrived at my room around midnight, my fellow officers had assembled in our communal living room to open the Christmas cards and packages they had received. One of the officers—from Tyler, Texas—had received a large shipping box, and we were all curious about its contents. It contained a smoked turkey! At Camp Nabors, we only ate turkey during Thanksgiving, so having turkey again, albeit smoked, was a fine ending to an otherwise long, sad day.

Four months before my tour in Korea was due to end, I applied to attend the 23-week Officer Advanced Course. The course trained officers to function as commanders and staff officers with the Army in the field. I wanted to attend this course because it was a requirement prior to advancement to the next, higher rank of major—my next stepping stone toward my goal of eventually becoming an Army colonel. I was selected and ordered to attend the course to be held at Fort Sam in January 1971. My wife was happy with this assignment; it would enable me to move with her into the house we had purchased in San Antonio prior to my departure to South Korea.

During the Officer Advanced Course, on June 25, 1971, my daughter Valerie was born. Her arrival brought immense happiness to my wife and me. Witnessing the miracle of a new life was a unique experience. Joy, profound love, and the realization of my new role as a father overwhelmed me. I worked as hard at being a father as I did during my training.

Prior to the completion of the course, I applied to the Patient Administration Course. This eight-week course prepared medical service corps officers in the management of medical information, aeromedical evacuation operations, and patient tracking and accountability. Completing this course would open the door for an assignment in an Army hospital. I was selected and began my studies in September 1971. Thankfully, the course was also held at Fort Sam, so I didn't need to leave my family.

MY FIRST HOSPITAL JOB

After successfully completing that course, I received my first hospital assignment at Valley Forge General Hospital in Phoenixville, Pennsylvania—the largest psychiatric hospital in the Army—as Chief of Admissions and Dispositions (AAD). I was extremely happy with this assignment. It was my entry-level job into healthcare administration and transitioned me from training Soldiers and working in field units into the hospital environment. My wife was excited as well. She had not traveled outside of Texas and saw this as an opportunity to visit cities on the East Coast.

Valley Forge was also the primary receiving hospital for repatriated prisoners of war (POWs) from South Vietnam. After arriving at McGuire Air Force Base in New Jersey, POWs were brought to Valley Forge for medical tests, reunification with their families, and readjustment to life in the U.S. Each POW worked with an officer who escorted them around the hospital and assisted them in their readjustment. I was selected as one of those officers. I escorted the last POW of the Vietnam War, Captain Robert (Bob) T. White. From our first encounter at the Air Force Base, we bonded by sharing our military experiences, going to dinner outside the hospital, and spending time with my family in my apartment.

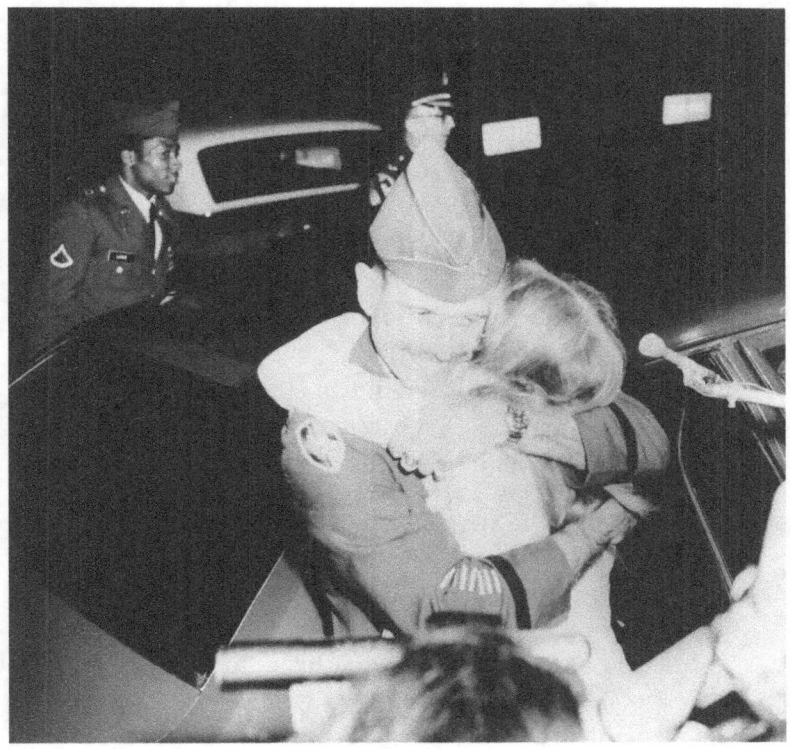

Image 17. Captain Robert T. White, a former Vietnam POW, welcomed upon his arrival at McGuire Air Force Base

For three months, I met with him every day, escorted him to his medical appointments, and explained what had happened in the U.S. since his imprisonment seven years before. My conversations and updates were eye-openers for him. On one occasion, I took him to a shopping mall. He marveled at the variety of stores and the products one could purchase. I patiently described to him the antiwar movement, national politics, and the most popular TV programs. He seemed enthralled by the changes that had taken place.

Hearing about his experiences as a POW in the jungles of South Vietnam was captivating. He had endured much hardship and isolation but never felt sorry for himself, and he didn't show any hatred toward others. It exemplified for me the strength of the human spirit—how one can overcome unfavorable circumstances with patience, determination, and the will to survive. His story continues to inspire me today.

At our last meeting, he gave me a pewter mug engraved with "JAKE, THANK YOU!" It wasn't until later that day that I noticed a piece of paper inside. The handwritten note said, "Jake: when the conversation turns to nice people, your name will always come to my mind. Bob White." His personalized gift and his thoughtfulness almost brought tears to my eyes.

After Bob's departure, I received a letter from the hospital commander, Colonel Phillip A. Deffer, expressing the following:

> I wish to commend you for your outstanding performance of duty as escort for CPT Robert T. White. You have successfully performed a duty far above and beyond the latitudes of your Military Occupational Specialty. You were thrust into an unfamiliar and sensitive situation on very short notice, and you performed marvelously. It is difficult for me to adequately express the depth of my pride in your accomplishments. On behalf of CPT White, his family, and the entire Operation Homecoming staff, I commend you for your unselfish, untiring, and devoted performance of duty. The entire operation could never have been carried out in a smooth and orderly manner without you.[3]

I appreciated Colonel Deffer's generous letter. I didn't expect it because I was merely doing my job.

ADMINISTRATIVE OFFICER

After Operation Homecoming, Valley Forge established the first alcohol and drug abuse treatment center in the Army. The treatment center included a military psychiatrist, nurses, civilian psychologists, and administrative staff. Colonel Deffer selected me as the treatment center's administrative officer, in addition to my other duties. Despite my lack of experience running a treatment center, my work as chief of AAD and escorting Captain White had demonstrated the skills desired for the center's administrator. I was proud of being selected because there were officers with more experience who could have assumed that role. I was determined to prove to Colonel Deffer that he made the right choice in picking me.

Prior to assuming my new role, I had to attend the recently established U.S. Army Drug and Alcohol Abuse Rehabilitation and Treatment course at Fort Sam. I would be part of its first class.

A SHOCKING ANNOUNCEMENT

After a few months as the center's administrator, the relative peace at Valley Forge was interrupted by the sudden announcement of the hospital's closure. I was shocked by the news! Valley Forge was one of the largest Army hospitals, with a proven reputation for providing excellent care. The announcement was devastating to the local community, who, many years earlier, had built the hospital, which was now a source of employment for many. It also upset our staff, who loved the hospital, its history, and its many accomplishments. The local people were angry at Valley Forge's closure and vented their feelings at the remaining staff.

My AAD office was the first point of entry into the hospital and became the main target of patients demanding answers and showing their irritation. I put my personal feelings aside and—using my powers of persuasion and understanding—listened to their complaints and deflected their justified anger.

During the drawdown, I transferred patients to other military facilities in Philadelphia and New Jersey and delivered the medical records of patients who resided in the local community. As the staff was reduced, the remaining officers assumed other duties. I was assigned several jobs, adding to my already stressful workday. I shifted from working five days a week to six, and from eight-hour days to ten-hour days. My son Jason was born in the middle of this upheaval, on August 15, 1973. His arrival was a joyous occasion for my wife and me. However, helping to take care of a newborn and working so many extra hours was stressful.

Two months after the announcement, Valley Forge's Chief of Military Personnel, Lieutenant Colonel Joseph DePonte, invited me to the Pentagon to discuss issues associated with the closure of Valley Forge, such as the reassignment of its military personnel. He suggested that, while there, I talk to my career management officer about a job in healthcare management. I had already given that a thought, so I agreed with his suggestion.

I had never visited the Pentagon and was instantly in awe of its gargantuan size. Divided into five wedges—with each wedge containing multiple offices, corridors, and walkways—it was easy to get lost in the building. At the Pentagon, we visited the Army Medical Department offices. While there, I saw my career management officer and mentioned that I wanted to manage a healthcare facility. He said he had a job for me at a clinic in New York. I asked for a couple of days to think about the offer because I wanted to learn more about the job, and he agreed.

During our return trip, however, I mentioned the New York job to Lieutenant Colonel DePonte. Arching his bushy eyebrows, he said, "Jake, don't take that job. That facility is also scheduled for closure." I was relieved because I did not want to go to another facility that was going to be closed.

COMING HOME

Back at Valley Forge, I called my career management officer and rejected the job offer. He immediately mentioned a similar position at a health clinic in Fort Buchanan, Puerto Rico. I could not believe my ears! I had regularly listed Puerto Rico as my primary choice of assignment, but after several unsuccessful attempts, I decided not to mention it again. I only had three weeks to tell my wife, pack our household goods, and move to Puerto Rico, but I didn't think twice about the offer—I accepted the job on the spot! I did not tell my parents about my new assignment, deciding, instead, to surprise them. This was one of the happiest days of my young Army career!

I left for Puerto Rico a couple of weeks before my family so I could report for duty and apply for housing at Fort Buchanan while my wife packed our household goods. When I arrived at the San Juan airport, I took public transportation to my parents' home. I barely had time to enjoy the scenery before we arrived, and I almost ran to their house. Walking on that familiar sidewalk was unreal. I couldn't believe that soon I would be telling my parents that for the next three years I was going to be living twenty-five miles away from them!

When I walked in, my dad, as usual, was in the living room listening to the radio and my mom was in the kitchen. When they saw me, they hugged me several times, then chastised me for not telling them that I was traveling to the island. When I told them I was staying in Puerto Rico for the next three years, they were ecstatic. My mom wanted to know when she would see her grandkids. My dad told me about the new fishing holes he had discovered, then planned visits to the townspeople who had followed my career from the news media and his updates.

Image 18. The author's parents, Juan Lozada and Clotilde Pereira

GRADUAL UPDATES

I spent four wonderful days with my parents, enjoying my mom's cooking and my dad's fishing trips, before traveling to Fort Buchanan, near San Juan. Upon arrival, I inquired about housing and was assigned a three-bedroom home approximately one mile from the clinic. With a three-year-old daughter and one-year-old son, the house, albeit small, met my family's needs.

I arrived at the health clinic and found obsolete medical and dental equipment and dissatisfied patients. I contacted the health clinic's headquarters on the mainland to report the situation. They informed me that they were aware of some of the problems and were also unhappy about the situation. Much work was needed to modernize the facility and restore the orderly functioning of the clinic. They were counting on me to see it through.

In addition to the outdated equipment, the clinic did not provide specialty care, such as pediatrics, orthopedics, and general surgery. It also did not provide healthcare after normal duty hours or on holidays and weekends. I was shocked! The condition of the clinic and the enormity of my task overwhelmed me. I wished I had accepted the New York job!

There was no way to do everything at once, so I focused on improving the quality of care first. I replaced one of the two physicians for refusing the work schedule I assigned to him and hired a nurse plus a highly qualified pharmacist to fill vacancies that had existed for three months. Next, I visited the hospital at the Roosevelt Roads Naval Base, near the town of Ceiba, because I knew they had medical and surgical specialists on staff. I met the hospital commander—a fine naval officer and physician from Beeville, Texas—and from the beginning, we hit it off well. With his support, I arranged for his staff to provide specialty care at Fort Buchanan once a week.

Then, I met with the commanders of the U.S. Army Reserve and National Guard medical units in Puerto Rico. They needed a facility to conduct their required monthly drills; I needed the support of their medical and surgical specialties.

We agreed that when my physicians needed X-rays read, we would send them to one of their radiologists. The radiologists would send the results and a report back to our clinic. In exchange, once a month, I allowed the medical units to perform physical exams and fulfill their monthly training requirements at the health clinic. During their monthly drills, they would conduct additional specialty clinics at the health clinic for my patients. With these partnerships in place, we'd already fixed many of Fort Buchanan's medical issues. But there was one more partnership I had in mind to fill other vacancies.

I wanted to leverage the VA Medical Center and local civilian hospitals to augment the services at the health clinic. I visited the medical center and met with its director. He was facing a big challenge. He needed help preventing Puerto Rican Soldiers on military leave from reporting sick to the hospital and staying too long without returning to their units on the mainland. This also created a problem for the military personnel office at Fort Buchanan. They had to support these Soldiers as if they were assigned to Fort Buchanan. I told him that I could solve this problem by returning the Soldiers to the mainland. All I needed was a medical statement declaring they were medically fit to travel by aircraft to their assignments. Two days later, the director sent me a list of names. I obtained orders from the military personnel office, arranged transportation, then informed the Soldiers that they would need to report the following Saturday to return to their assigned units.

The day after the notifications went out, a group of gloomy and upset parents, wives, and girlfriends flooded the clinic. Some carried statements from family physicians and local clergy stating the need for the Soldiers to remain in Puerto Rico. I read all of them and listened to everyone carefully. At the end, I explained why the Soldiers could not remain in Puerto Rico and provided the procedures to apply for a discharge from the Army if they qualified for hardship conditions. I sympathized with the Soldiers' desire to stay in Puerto Rico; however, they had made a commitment with the Army and couldn't remain on the island.

The following Monday, the VA Medical Center director called to thank me. During the conversation, he asked if there was anything he could do to help me. I had been hoping he would make this offer, so I mentioned two things. First, I needed specialized laboratory testing for cases like hemophilia, and ultrasound support. Second, we needed specialty care for those patients Roosevelt Roads could not handle. He agreed to both. I was elated by the agreement; it solved two of my pressing problems at the clinic.

FINDING AFTER-HOURS CARE

The civilian hospitals provided the biggest challenge because I did not know anyone in the local healthcare sector. Luckily, I was invited to the monthly meeting of the San Juan healthcare administrators, where I met Mr. Jesús M. Rodríguez, an Army Reserve officer and senior healthcare administrator at one of the civilian hospitals. Mr. Rodríguez needed a military medical facility to conduct his required training because he was unable to travel to the mainland. Seeing this as an opportunity to establish a connection with the civilian medical community, I suggested he complete his required training at the health clinic.

During the first few days of his training, I learned he was the administrator of Presbyterian Hospital, one of the most reputable healthcare facilities in San Juan. As we got to know each other better, I toured his hospital many times, he visited my clinic, and we had dinner often. We developed a close relationship that led to an agreement. My patients would receive after-hours emergency care from his hospital on a reimbursable basis.

After much effort—and with the support of the VA Medical Center, the Naval Hospital at Roosevelt Roads, the Presbyterian Hospital, the U.S. Army Reserve and National Guard medical units, and my headquarters in Georgia, as well as the Fort Buchanan military personnel office and Scott Air Force Base aeromedical evacuation staff—I developed a comprehensive healthcare delivery system for the Soldiers and their families at Fort Buchanan. It took four months to make specialties such as orthopedics, pediatrics, internal medicine, and specialized laboratory testing available to the patients at Fort Buchanan.

TWO INITIATIVES

In addition to running the clinic, I was also the advisor for the Civilian Health and Medical Program of the Uniformed Services (CHAMPUS) in Puerto Rico. CHAMPUS was a Department of Defense program that reimbursed Soldiers for authorized care provided by medical facilities in the private sector. The CHAMPUS advisor role was the most time consuming. It required many hours explaining to patients and healthcare providers the intricacies of the program.

Most of the CHAMPUS beneficiaries on the island, including the Puerto Rican spouses of military personnel, had limited command of the English language and encountered tremendous difficulty navigating the program. They struggled to understand the bureaucratic terms on the reimbursement forms as well as the CHAMPUS instruction manual.

To help them, I developed two initiatives. First, I cross-trained Mrs. Epstein, my bilingual secretary, and appointed her the CHAMPUS assistant advisor. As such, she was able to counsel beneficiaries and help them file their reimbursement forms. Second, I translated the CHAMPUS forms and instruction manuals into Spanish. It took a couple of weeks to print the forms and pamphlets into Spanish, but these initiatives reduced the CHAMPUS backlog. Beneficiaries completed the CHAMPUS forms more quickly, and the local healthcare providers received their reimbursements sooner. Overall, everyone involved in the program was pleased.

MUCH IMPROVED

Next, I tackled the appearance of the clinic. Patients did not have a separate waiting area from the emergency room, the walls were faded, and the floors were scuffed. My senior NCO was a good carpenter, and after extensive conversations with my headquarters, I obtained the funds to update the building.

Remodeling was not easy. We had to work between patients and maximize weekends and holidays. Each Soldier (including me) voluntarily pitched in. In a couple of months, we built a new waiting area, painted the interior with harmonized colors, added decorative panels to some of the walls, and scrubbed and rewaxed the floors. After a lot of hard work, we had a much improved and better-looking facility!

EXTRA TASKS

Another challenge I encountered was having two bosses (Colonel Josiah Wallace, an Infantry officer and Fort Buchanan commander) and Brigadier General John W. White (the commanding general of Eisenhower Army Medical Center in Augusta, Georgia).

Colonel Wallace had allegedly derailed a few officers' careers because he was demanding and hard to please. He obsessed over possible military conflicts in the Caribbean and Fort Buchanan's role in those conflicts. He scheduled numerous meetings about military readiness, as well as monthly briefings to demonstrate progress. I had to track every statistic related to the clinic, including how many patients had been seen, the number of procedures performed, and how many patients had been transported to other facilities. These extra tasks added several hours to my busy work schedule each week.

It was not easy to work with limited resources thousands of miles away from headquarters and meet the desires of a highly demanding local boss. The orders and requests from my two bosses sometimes overlapped, forcing me to complete one project late or work overtime to meet both deadlines. I learned quickly that the best way to develop a good working relationship with Colonel Wallace was to support his priorities and maintain good statistics about the clinic. When he saw me prioritizing his requests and giving him statistics on time, he relaxed his deadlines on other projects, letting me meet the expectations of both bosses.

Despite the bureaucratic challenges, the needs of our patients came first. When we started remodeling the clinic, my nurse reported an upset patient who did not have transportation for an appointment at a civilian hospital. I walked into the waiting area and saw a young pregnant woman distraught and almost in tears. She thought the health clinic provided transportation. She was so upset at missing her appointment that I offered to take her in my car. Her eyes lit up and she accepted. I didn't see my offer to provide transportation as a hardship; I was happy to do this for a patient who needed help.

A few days later, I met Specialist Droz, Colonel Wallace's driver. After he introduced himself, he said, "My wife was upset about missing an appointment at a local hospital and you went out of your way to help her. She told me all about it and I mentioned it to the colonel. I know of his reputation, but he was so impressed about what you did that I believe you will be fine!"

Improving Relationships

Colonel Wallace also fixated on the landscaping of Fort Buchanan. Once a month, he required all military personnel to assemble in front of the headquarters building for a day of clearing culverts, planting bushes, and trimming trees. On one particularly muggy day, the chief of the inspector general's office became ill from heat exhaustion. He was fatigued, dizzy, and sweating heavily. He was helped to the health clinic, and we were able to take care of him. I had the unpleasant task of informing Colonel Wallace. He saw red and immediately postponed the project until everyone was trained about how to prevent and treat heat illnesses.

Initially, he wanted to include my Soldiers in his landscaping projects. I convinced him that they should be spared because I would have to close the clinic. Realizing he would be inundated with complaints from Fort Buchanan residents, he begrudgingly excluded my staff. I, in turn, agreed to maintain the area around the health clinic in accordance with his standards.

One rainy Sunday, Colonel Wallace called and asked me to report to his house in work clothes. "We are going to look for additional plants for the health clinic," he said. When I arrived, he was already in his station wagon with a couple of shovels and hoes in the trunk. I climbed in and we took off. It was raining cats and dogs when we drove around the post looking for plants. Wherever he saw a plant he liked, he would direct me to dig it out and put it in the trunk. A couple of hours later, he drove to the health clinic, where he gave me detailed instructions for planting them. Exhausted, wet, and covered with mud, I finished his bizarre project. This awkward experience improved my relationship with Colonel Wallace. He saw that I was willing to follow his lead without objections, so he trusted me more and stopped micromanaging the clinic.

Our move to Puerto Rico immersed my wife in a new culture, language, and set of customs. As time passed, the initial excitement faded, and homesickness crept in. She missed her established social network, familiar comforts, close friends, and the seasonal changes of home.

MY BIG BOSS'S VISIT

When Brigadier General White made his first trip to the health clinic, I coordinated a trip to the Navy hospital. As we approached the town of Luquillo, he marveled at the turquoise-green rolling waves of the beach alongside the road. We were ahead of schedule, so I offered to take him swimming. I had brought two swimsuits in the car, so he happily agreed and borrowed one. For the next forty-five minutes, he enjoyed the warm waters and the salty air of Luquillo beach.

The time we spent at the beach helped me develop a good relationship with General White. I was able to share, in a relaxed setting, details about my family, my early years in Puerto Rico, and my career. I also listed the challenges I faced at the clinic and some of the improvements we had already made. The general became less stern, moving my relationship from professional to personal.

The following day, I took the general to Colonel Wallace's office. The colonel was not a flattering individual, so I was bowled over when he complimented my work and listed the changes I had made at the clinic. After this visit, I took General White to the health clinic to meet my staff. Most of them had never met an Army general. Most importantly, they were thrilled to meet our "big boss" from the mainland. My staff circled around him, introducing themselves, welcoming the general to the clinic, and asking questions. It was a great visit! Prior to his departure, General White committed his support to the clinic and appointed a member of his staff as his point of contact in case I needed help.

Image 19. The author with Brigadier General John W. White at Luquillo Beach

Seven months after arriving at Fort Buchanan, we learned that a colonel from headquarters would be arriving to close the dental clinic. Closing it would be disastrous to our beneficiaries— it would force them to travel two hours to the naval base to receive dental care or see civilian dentists at their own expense. I explained these hardships in a brief I planned to present to the visiting colonel.

When the colonel landed, I scheduled a trip to the naval base. Heavy traffic delayed our two-hour trip by forty-five minutes. Upon arrival, my visitor was exhausted and carsick. Nauseous and dizzy as we approached the clinic, he asked why I had brought him there. I said, "Sir, I wanted you to experience what my patients will have to go through if we don't have a dental clinic at Fort Buchanan."

On our way back to San Juan, he thanked me profusely for the briefing. He also thanked me for illustrating the difficulties our patients would face if they had to travel to the naval base. Instead of announcing the closure of our dental clinic, he decided to modernize it so we could better support our patients! A month later, we received two new dental chairs, equipment, and much-needed supplies. In addition, I received funding to maintain our equipment and to allow our staff to attend training courses on the mainland. I couldn't have been happier!

We received even more support after Major General Spurgeon Neel, the commanding general of the Health Services Command in San Antonio, visited Puerto Rico to attend a National Guard event. I knew I could not waste the opportunity to introduce him to our clinic and other military medical units on the island, so I developed a full week's itinerary for him. The schedule included visits to the U.S. Army Reserve and National Guard medical units, the Naval Hospital, and our health clinic. I sent the proposed itinerary to the general's aide. The general was so impressed by the itinerary that he accepted it without change. After his return to the mainland, he contacted General

White to request that I receive the resources needed to support my patients.

I was happy about the turn of events. For too long, the health clinic had functioned with antiquated equipment, despite the recent funding. We were able to modernize it and provide better care for our patients. Years later, whenever I saw Major General Neel, he would mention that the trip to Puerto Rico had been one of the most enjoyable in his entire Army career!

During the next six months, life was much easier at Fort Buchanan. I continued to receive the supplies and equipment I needed, as well as the funding to pay the VA hospital for laboratory support. Our patients were satisfied, and the morale of my staff was high.

The end of my three-year assignment at Fort Buchanan was approaching when I received word that Brigadier General White was going to visit us again. He had been extremely supportive after his first visit and had granted me practically every request I had submitted. During this visit, the general gathered my staff and listed my accomplishments and the great progress we had made in creating an efficient healthcare system so far away from the mainland. After he finished, he awarded me an Army Commendation Medal. I was speechless and extremely touched by the general's recognition. Pride filled my chest while I stood at attention as he made the presentation. To be recognized in front of my staff meant a lot to me. All the hard work and dedication had really paid off.

After the general's visit, more great news followed. I learned that I had been selected for promotion to the rank of major. I would leave the ranks of junior officers to join the senior officers' ranks, which included an increase in pay and better on-post housing. I could not hide my excitement and immediately shared the great news with my family and the clinic's staff.

More great news followed. I had applied to attend the U.S. Army-Baylor Program in Healthcare Administration and learned that I was selected. This highly competitive two-year program was a stepping stone to future leadership assignments in the military healthcare system. Held at Fort Sam, only eighteen officers from the entire U.S. Army were chosen. Upon graduation, officers received a master's degree in healthcare administration from Baylor University.

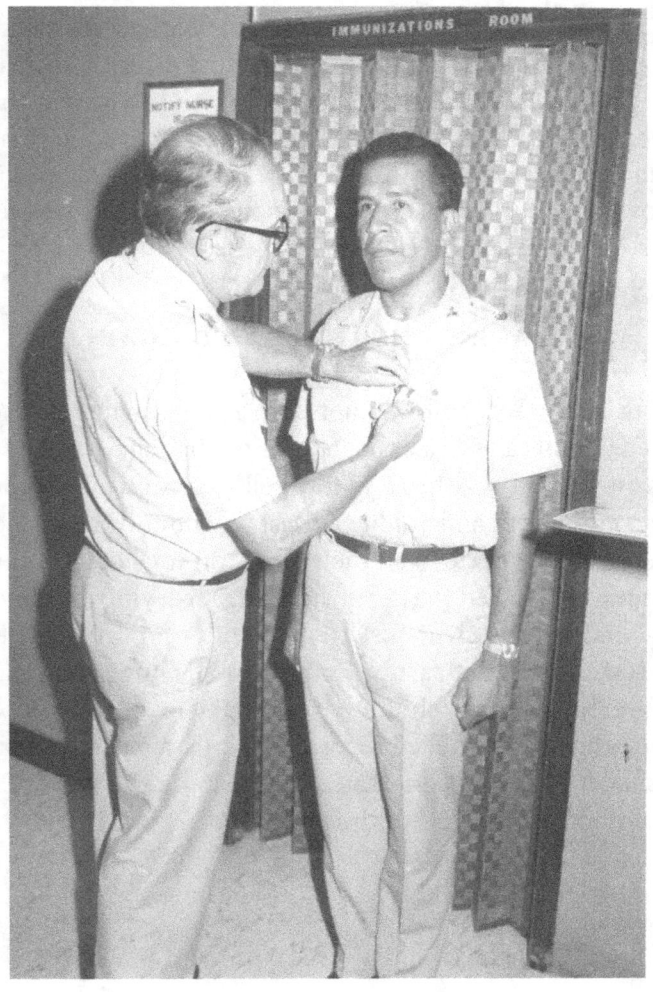

Image 20. Brigadier General White awards the author the Army Commendation Medal

Puerto Rico had been a tough assignment. My dad best summed up the many hours and hard work required by remarking, "Son, I saw more of you when you lived on the mainland than when you lived at Fort Buchanan."

Despite the difficulties, and with the help of my staff, I had transformed the health clinic into a superb healthcare facility, reducing the number of complaints from Soldiers, their families, and patients to practically zero. I also forged relationships with other military medical organizations on the island, at the VA Medical Center, and in the private sector. These relationships helped me succeed in my first healthcare administrator's job. As a fellow officer said, "Jake, you have become the Army Medical Department's most trusted representative in Puerto Rico!"

Leaving the Homeland Again

Leaving Fort Buchanan was not easy. I was leaving behind my beloved parents and a healthcare facility I had modernized from the ground up. I was bidding farewell to a motivated group of civilian employees and Soldiers, most of whom I'd recruited and trained and who performed their jobs with total dedication.

In July 1974, I left the health clinic. After saying my goodbyes to my Soldiers and civilian staff, my family and I traveled to my hometown where, with a lump in my throat, I hugged my parents goodbye. My wife and children were happy to return to Texas. I, on the other hand, looked forward with great anticipation to a new challenge as a postgraduate student in the U.S. Army-Baylor Program in Healthcare Administration.

CHAPTER 5

RISING THROUGH THE RANKS

UPON ARRIVAL AT FORT SAM, I LEARNED THAT THERE WERE no houses available on post, so my wife and I had to purchase one. I contacted a Realtor, and we were able to find a nice three-bedroom home approximately thirty minutes from Fort Sam.

A couple of days after moving into our new home, I reported to the Academy of Health Sciences (AHS) to begin the Army-Baylor program. My class consisted of thirty-four officers from the Army, Navy, Air Force, and VA. Year one would include intense academic work, followed by a one-year residency at a hospital or major healthcare organization. I discussed the demanding academic requirements with my family. We agreed that I would dedicate Friday evenings to family activities and the rest of my time to research, writing papers, and group study sessions.

Maintaining open and honest communication was essential for my wife to understand the academic requirements of the Army/Baylor Program. By actively engaging with me and learning about the specific challenges I faced, she was able to set realistic expectations and offer meaningful support throughout this demanding period of our lives. This collaborative approach fostered a strong partnership and ensured we navigated the program's intensity together.

The first day of class proceeded uneventfully until the director of the program walked hurriedly to where I was sitting. "Major Lozada, I've been informed that Major General Neel wants you to stop by his office. Is there a particular reason why he wants to see you?"

My reply was quick. "Sir, I don't know why General Neel wants to see me."

"If I were you, I would go see him right away," he replied.

I hurried to the Health Services Command headquarters building across the street from AHS, where General Neel asked me to follow him to an office. As we entered, he said, "Do you know why I wanted to see you?"

"No, Sir," I replied.

"When we first met, my personal aide was being transferred, and I needed a replacement. After meeting you in Puerto Rico, I concluded that you were the best candidate to take his position. I subsequently learned that you had been selected to attend the Baylor program. Attending the program would be better for your Army career, so I didn't ask for you to be my aide. Nevertheless, I wanted you to see the office you would have occupied."

I was so moved by General Neel's gesture that I was unable to get a word out. Considering me as his top candidate for the aide's job was a tremendous compliment.

ACADEMICS

Most of my Baylor classmates already had master's degrees and experience researching and writing term papers. I did not. That gave them an advantage and made things easier for them. I, on the other hand, did not have a master's degree and had no experience writing term papers. Our term papers had to be typed following specific formats and standards. I found a great typist not too far from my home to help. When I finished handwriting each paper, I dropped it in her mailbox. By noon of the following day, the paper was typewritten flawlessly.

The academic program was extremely difficult. The instructors gave us long reading assignments and tough homework daily. There was never enough time to complete the academic work. Every evening, after having dinner with my family, I locked myself in my home office and studied until midnight. I joined a student study group that met weekly to complete group assignments.

Despite the program's time-consuming requirements, I found time to participate in athletic activities. I was both a player and a coach of the students' volleyball and basketball teams, and I played softball against the faculty. These activities gave my mind a break from the academic environment. They also helped me establish good relationships with my classmates and the faculty.

Near the end of the first year, we were asked to list our top choices for our residency. I chose Brooke Army Medical Center (at Fort Sam) and Dwight D. Eisenhower Army Medical Center at Fort Gordon, Georgia as my first and second choices. I preferred Brooke Army Medical Center because I wouldn't have to move my family. Dwight D. Eisenhower Army Medical Center was my higher headquarters when I was at Fort Buchanan, and I already knew its commander, General White, and its staff. I was not disappointed when I was given my second choice.

I met my residency preceptor, Colonel Marion P. Johnson, during the final stages of year one of the program. Soft-spoken, efficient, and kind, the executive officer at the medical center had a reputation as one of the best hospital administrators in the Army. During one of his visits to Fort Sam, I invited him home for dinner so he could meet my family, and so we could get to know each other better. During dinner, he discussed my residency requirements and his expectations of me. The time we spent together laid the groundwork for a friendship that has lasted for decades.

On July 7, 1978, my family joined me in Willis Hall Auditorium for our graduation. Top officials from Baylor University and senior officers from the AHS were also present. We had endured a grueling academic year and were returning to a normal environment without homework assignments, exams, and study sessions. My family was proud of me and happy to have me back without the pressures and stress of the course. After graduation, we celebrated by going out to dinner at a local restaurant. On September 26, I received my academic report:

> Major Lozada was truly an outstanding student and officer throughout this demanding graduate program. His responses to each of the many course requirements demonstrated his maturity, alacrity, and keen intelligence. He possesses the potential for a highly successful career in the Army Medical Department. He is recommended for Command and General Staff College.[1]

The Command and General Staff College course was a stepping stone to another promotion to the rank of Lieutenant Colonel. It developed leaders for military operations in multinational operational environments. This was a military course that all officers with my rank and experience wanted to complete.

Georgia

A couple of weeks later, my family and I made the two-day trip to Fort Gordon in Augusta, Georgia, in two cars. One of them didn't have air-conditioning. I rode in this car with the blistering summer heat of the south almost melting the asphalt. After settling into a three-bedroom home on post, I reported to the medical center, where I was assigned an office in the command suite. Having an office near Colonel Johnson and General White was an additional benefit; it allowed me to closely interact with them and other senior staff members.

The medical center was a welcome change from the stressful academic environment of the Baylor program. Having Colonel Johnson as my preceptor was a true blessing because he allowed me to delve into administrative as well as clinical areas of the medical center and observe his work as a senior healthcare executive. Our preceptors were healthcare leaders who served as mentors to the students during the second year of the Baylor program. Many were alumni of the program.

Augusta had excellent private sector hospitals and a VA medical center. As part of the residency, I visited multiple healthcare facilities, paying particular attention to the differences and commonalities among them. I had to write detailed reports of the visits, listing the lessons I learned. Every quarter, I had to submit them to the Baylor faculty for review and approval. Between these visits and Colonel Johnson's leadership, I learned, firsthand, the role of a medical center administrator. That experience prepared me to someday run my own hospital.

Near the end of my residency, it was again time to call my career management officer to discuss my next assignment. He offered me three choices: Chief of Patient Administration at the U.S. Army Hospital in Heidelberg, Germany; a staff job in the Office of the Surgeon General in the Pentagon; or Inspector General (IG) at Health Services Command. The high-visibility job in the Pentagon would enhance my career, but the cost of living in Washington, DC, was extremely high. Heidelberg was an exciting choice, but I was persuaded by my wife, whose family lived in Houston, to take the IG job. It required a lot of travel, but my wife loved Texas, and returning to San Antonio seemed to be the least disruptive move. The IG job was challenging, but it provided a unique opportunity to increase my knowledge of healthcare management and administration.

The HSC IG team evaluated the health, dental, and veterinary activities of the Army Medical Department in the continental U.S., Panama, Alaska, and Puerto Rico. It also inspected the Academy of Health Sciences at Fort Sam. The team included 10-12 permanent inspectors, including nurses, dentists, veterinarians, and comptrollers, augmented by other specialists. My duties included inspecting patient administration areas: admissions and dispositions (discharges) of patients, management and accountability of patients, management of medical records, and biostatistics, among others. I also inspected the health clinics outside the hospitals and other professional services. My work schedule was always tight because some of the health clinics were in remote locations.

Being an IG was stressful. We traveled every other week and had to be experts in the areas we inspected. We were seen as a threat to those we inspected because job performance evaluations were sometimes based on the results of our inspections. Some trips were very enjoyable though. In Alaska, I traveled to different Army sites and learned much about our "last frontier." Its arctic plains and mountain peaks, dusted with snow, were a sight to behold. My two-week trip to Panama gave me the opportunity to explore the Panama Canal during the weekend.

Yet while I appreciated the chance to explore new places, each trip was—at its heart—a work trip, and those had their own complications. For example, the Panama inspection took place as the U.S. government was transferring control of the Panama Canal to the Panamanian government. There was a palpable unease and a strained mood when we arrived—one could feel the tension in the air. Because of the political tension, we were advised not to wear our uniforms outside our hotels.

Learning, Learning ...

Halfway through our inspection of the Army hospital at Fort Stewart, Georgia, the Army announced the list of officers selected for promotion to Lieutenant Colonel. I made the list, but a colleague on our IG team did not. The news of his non-selection put a damper on mine—I had to keep my excitement under control in front of the team, making the rest of the week uncomfortable for me because I knew how devastated he felt.

Although the IG job was stressful, becoming a functional expert in the administration of healthcare facilities, staying current on healthcare policies and regulations, and inspecting multiple facilities prepared me for advancement in and out of the Army. It also gave me the rare opportunity to learn how different healthcare facilities functioned, how quality healthcare could be measured and delivered, and how good leadership could make a difference in managing highly complex organizations. I used that knowledge and experience at my next assignment as commander of the 8th Combat Support Hospital at Fort Ord, California. A springboard to becoming a colonel, I happily accepted the assignment when it was offered to me by my career counselor.

Super 8!

Fort Ord, located on the Monterey Peninsula, was home to the 7th Infantry Division, and its commanding general would become the senior rater on my performance evaluation. Living near the beautiful city of Carmel was a big plus for my family. They had access to its beautiful surroundings, the picturesque 17-mile drive and the Pacific Coast with its mountainous coastline, beaches, and harbors. The city of San Francisco, which my family and I enjoyed visiting, was only two hours away. I would use my four years of IG experience to strengthen the clinical and administrative functions of the combat support hospital, but I also looked forward to leading Soldiers again.

The hospital had a small but highly efficient group of officers and an outstanding group of NCOs. The highest-ranking NCO was First Sergeant Pedrigo Regala, born and reared in the Philippines, and one of the toughest but most caring NCOs I had ever known. On most Sundays, he would walk through the barracks and invite Soldiers to the Fort Ord movie theater—all expenses paid by him. For my Soldiers, whose salaries were low, this was a special act of kindness.

Image 21. The author assuming command of the 8th Combat Support Hospital

During my two-year command, our unit deployed multiple times on field training exercises to fine-tune Soldiers' skills and test our field equipment. The deployments tested my skills at planning and executing complex missions in a field environment.

While deployed, we used inflatable shelters to set up our 200-bed hospital. Auxiliary power units provided air-conditioning and kept the shelters inflated. Expandable shelters created the operating rooms, pharmacy, laboratory, and administrative areas.

Maintaining the inflatable units was an enormous undertaking. They developed tears constantly, requiring patching with a difficult-to-apply special glue. Their plastic panels, with their glossy surfaces radiating heat, added to the challenge of maintaining a comfortable environment. To cool the units, I decided to spread water over them with garden hoses. The idea worked well, lowering the inside temperature of the units.

During our deployments, the hospital staff size doubled by adding clinical staff from the Silas B. Hayes Army Hospital at Fort Ord. There was a reason for this growth. When our field hospital was not deployed, our permanent staff maintained our equipment and engaged in training to ensure proficiency in individual and collective tasks. However, during our deployments, additional personnel—including nurses, physicians, and ancillary staff—was needed to fully staff the 200-bed hospital. Invariably, I had to develop training programs to help the incoming staff adjust to our unit and the field environment.

After our unit returned from one training exercise, I challenged my staff to pursue the Expert Field Medical Badge (EFMB). The EFMB recognizes exceptional competence by medical personnel. Candidates are tested at all hours during a three-day field training exercise with very little sleep. The most difficult events were a three-hour written test and a 12-mile walk/run in all types of terrain to be completed wearing full field gear while carrying a rifle. One of the most challenging Army badges to earn, fewer than twenty percent of individuals who apply earn it. I motivated my staff to apply by volunteering myself to be tested. I was motivated by the challenge and the need to set an example for my Soldiers. Eight staff members volunteered. I developed a training program emphasizing multiple aspects of field medicine. We practiced and trained daily for two months.

The testing day arrived, and we were ready! The pace throughout the test was relentless, and we had very little rest. Different tactical situations required us to accomplish multiple tasks, including calling for medevac helicopters to evacuate casualties, treat casualties, and administer first aid. The test was tougher than I expected, but I did well in all events. I had trained thoroughly, including doing the 12-mile walk/run a couple of times in the allotted time.

It was exciting to see our families assembled at the end of the twelve miles, wildly cheering and clapping as we approached the finish line. Exhausted, we lined up—in military formation—to be awarded the highly coveted EFMB by our brigade commander. When he pinned the badge on my chest, I could not conceal my enormous pride in my staff; every candidate from our unit passed the test.

Several weeks after the EFMB test, our hospital was reconfigured into a 400-bed evacuation hospital. This change added additional inflatable units and expandable shelters, medical equipment, vehicles, supplies, and staff. Absorbing and training our growing staff was difficult, as they had not worked in a field environment. I helped the new staff members adjust to their latest environment by establishing a training program to show them how to maintain their field equipment and perform their assigned tasks in the field.

I led our 400-bed hospital during several deployments by air and ground to exercises in the California and Texas deserts. During one of these deployments, we successfully tested the capabilities of our newly established evacuation hospital. Transporting our Soldiers, equipment, and supplies was a huge undertaking. It required us to coordinate the use of ground transportation, rail, and military aircraft. Lieutenant Yolanda Matos, a young female officer, who coordinated the transportation of our hospital surprised me in the best way. She did a superb job with very little training and Army experience. These exercises improved our readiness in case of a deployment to a war zone. They also motivated our Soldiers to reach new heights.

Image 22. The 8th Combat Support Hospital during military training exercises

My Soldiers captured many awards, individually and as a unit, during my time in California. One of my Soldiers, Sergeant Jennifer Craig, was selected Soldier of the year, competing against more than 7,000 Soldiers assigned to Fort Ord. She was the only female among the group of twelve finalists. Another Soldier, on her own accord, designed and sewed a special flag for the hospital. She did such a great job that I ordered the construction of a flagpole in front of our building and proudly hoisted the flag during our morning military formations. Our 400-bed evacuation hospital, known as "Super 8," became one of the top units at Fort Ord!

BACK TO TEXAS

Sadly, my command tour was ending and I again had to contact my career management officer to negotiate my next assignment. I hated to leave the Monterey area and "Super 8," but mine was a two-year assignment. There were few challenging jobs in healthcare administration available, so I chose to return to Fort Sam as the chief of the Force Structure, Realignments, Security, and Intelligence Branch at HSC. My family was excited about returning to Texas.

Transitioning from an exciting field command into a staff job was heartbreaking. Instead of leading Soldiers, deploying to challenging locations, and overseeing field training exercises, I now had a desk job in a large bureaucracy, with lots of paperwork and administrative actions. Most of these actions entailed approving or disapproving organizational changes submitted by HSC subordinate organizations.

On May 16, 1985, the pace of my new job was interrupted by awe-inspiring news. My hometown had selected my mom as "Mother of the Year." The award was the highest recognition bestowed upon an individual in my hometown. Government leaders, key members of the community, church officials, and her many friends attended the award ceremony at the Lions Club. According to the citation, she had been selected for "gaining the respect, admiration, and love of her fellow townspeople; her excellent work on behalf of San Lorenzo; her church leadership; and especially her support of the most disadvantaged."

Several days later, Mom was recognized again at an event in San Juan. Our entire family was thrilled! My mom's neighbors and her church's members were euphoric about the well-deserved recognitions. It had been a long journey for my mom from the cold mountains of Guayama—where, as a child, she slept on a mattress made from dried plantain leaves—to being recognized publicly as Mother of the Year!

I was not able to attend these events, but my dad painstakingly shared every detail. A few months later, I took a short vacation to my parents' home and was able to congratulate my mother in person. As always, I went fishing with my dad and my youngest brother. On one of our fishing trips, my dad looked unusually run-down and pallid. I mentioned it to him, and he agreed to see a physician. A couple of weeks after my return home, I called to check on him. He was diagnosed with aplastic anemia—his body had stopped producing new blood cells. I called a retired military hematologist friend of mine in Humacao, who agreed to treat him, but his condition did not improve. Ten months later, I went to see him again. When I arrived, my dad was in a lot of pain, but he said, "The family is now complete."

The following morning, my mom, my youngest brother, and I took him to a hospital in San Juan for some testing. After being admitted, my mom and my brother left to bring lunch. While they were gone, my dad asked me for a cup of coffee, which my mom had brought in a thermos. When my back was turned, he took a sip and said, "Your mom makes the best coffee in the world." When I turned back around, his eyes were fixed, his pupils no longer responsive to light. I ran to find a nurse, who checked him and told me my dear dad was dead.

I was in total shock and despair and had difficulty processing what was happening. I ran to the parking lot to wait for my mom and my brother. As I waited, every minute seemed like an eternity. When they arrived, I shared the terrible news. We were all devastated! My mom could not believe what was happening, and my brother and I were in tears. We returned to the hospital in silence to arrange for the disposition of my dad's remains. After this painful process, we returned to my parents' home and barely spoke as we planned my dad's funeral.

After his funeral, I researched the causes of aplastic anemia to try to figure out how my dad could have contracted this illness. After much research, I learned that toxic chemicals in pesticides and insecticides had been linked to this disease. My dad would spread these chemicals to kill pests and insects in our yard, but he never wore protective gear. It was heartbreaking to realize that his love for gardening may have caused his death.

DISAPPOINTING NEWS

I was still mourning my dad's passing when the Army convened a selection board to consider officers for promotion to colonel. Although the probability of an officer reaching the rank of colonel (from their entry into active duty as a second lieutenant in the Army) was approximately 2 percent, I felt confident about my selection. I had successfully graduated from the Army-Baylor program and completed the U.S. Army Command and General Staff College. In addition, I had completed two of the most challenging and career-enhancing assignments at the lieutenant colonel level: Inspector General and Field Hospital Commander. I had punched all the tickets.

Despite my accomplishments, when the list of selectees was released, my boss, Colonel George Wahl, had the unfortunate task of informing me that I had not been selected. My decades of hard work and expectations were shattered. In addition to being labeled a "passed over," there was considerable bias against officers not selected for promotion—it also opened the door to be reassigned to the worst jobs available. Good jobs were often given to officers with promising careers and those who were "passed over" were not looked upon favorably.

Soldiers react differently to non-selection for promotion. Some get so upset that their career aspirations and enthusiasm take a sudden turn for the worse—feeling betrayed, they immediately apply for retirement. Others blame their performance evaluation raters for their misfortune. Others redouble their efforts to increase their chances of being promoted during the next selection board. I fell into the third group. My career objective was to achieve the rank of colonel, and nothing was going to deter me from achieving my goal. I knew that I had to put my nose to the grindstone and redouble my efforts.

My family was also confident of my selection for promotion, so it was difficult to share the bad news with them. They took the news hard and were immensely disappointed and upset. Keeping my emotions in check, I informed them that, even though I had an excellent chance of being hired as a healthcare administrator in the private sector, I was not going to apply for retirement. My goal was to be promoted to colonel in the U.S. Army!

The day after I learned of my non-selection, Colonel Wahl discussed how to enhance my chances for promotion. He offered to get me a job as primary Health Services Systems Manager at the AHS at Fort Sam. I happily agreed, and three weeks later I was reassigned. Colonel Wahl also recommended me for membership in the Order of Military Medical Merit. This private association recognized excellence, good fellowship, pride, and fellowship among Army Medical Department personnel.

Major General Tracey E. Strevey, Jr., president of the Order, sent me an acceptance letter stating, "I know that you will continue to contribute to the U.S. Army Medical Department in the manner of excellence that led you to your acceptance.[2] Colonel Wahl's recommendation and General Strevey's letter further reinforced my decision to stay in the Army and pursue the rank of colonel.

In my new job, I collected, organized, and presented information of impact on the combat readiness of the Army Medical Department to its senior leadership, Army leadership, and Department of Defense staff. My new boss was Colonel Timothy Jackman, a reputable MSC officer. I reported to him but interacted often with the AHS commandant (commander), Major General Alcide M. LaNoue. An intelligent and demanding officer, I knew of him decades before when he worked at the orthopedics department at Valley Forge General Hospital. Working directly for General LaNoue would improve my career and potential for promotion—receiving a good rating by a general officer could influence the selection committee more than a rating from a lower-ranking officer.

On May 3, 1989, after planning a one-day series of important briefings, I received a letter of appreciation from General LaNoue. The last sentence caught my eye. "The fine briefings you presented proved to be highly useful to me. With the quality of officer that you exemplify supporting the Academy, my job becomes much easier."[3]

Image 23. The author is awarded the Meritorious Service Medal

While at the AHS, I continued to search for a different job that would help me get promoted. That opportunity came in March 1989, when I was offered the job of executive officer (COO) of the 121st Evacuation Hospital/U.S. Army Hospital in Seoul, Korea. Once again, my family could not accompany me on the one-year assignment. The job would enhance my military record, though, so after consulting with my family, I accepted it, knowing I could visit home again in six months.

I arrived at the Kimpo Airport in Seoul, South Korea, after an exhausting flight from Texas. As we traveled to the military compound in Yongsan, the country did not look the same as it did in 1968. Gone was the heavy pollution, men and women pulling heavy-laden vegetable carts, and dilapidated housing. Modern high-rise buildings, fancy restaurants, and new hotels filled the city. The number of U.S. troops in the country had decreased.

At Yongsan, I shared a two-bedroom house with Major Ismael "Ish" Nuño, a thoracic surgeon. We became good friends and spent countless hours listening to Spanish music and enjoying the Mexican food I often cooked. Though he was a major, he knew very little about the military because he had been recruited as an officer for his medical experience. I taught him the various customs and traditions of the Army, as well as how to wear our uniforms.

I worked in an office adjacent to the hospital commander, Colonel James Peake—the hardest-working military officer I knew. He arrived at work around five in the morning, then visited the emergency room, patient wards, and other areas. By seven, when he hosted the daily morning report meeting with the chief nurse, chief of clinical services, and me, he was full of questions. We had to be on our toes and ready to answer without delay.

One of the highlights of my tour in Korea was a visit from the Army Surgeon General, Lieutenant General Frank F. Ledford. I met him when I was an IG and he, as a colonel, was the commander of the hospital in Fort Riley, Kansas. During his visit, I invited him to join Major Nuño and me for an evening of Mexican nachos and margaritas. Having the most senior officer in the Army Medical Department as my personal guest gave me the tremendous opportunity to share about my job and experiences in Korea, as well as my career plans.

Image 24. The author with Lieutenant General Frank F. Ledford, the Army Surgeon General, during the Army Surgeon General's visit to South Korea

AT LAST—COLONEL!

I had been in Korea several months when the Army convened another promotion board. Day after day, I anxiously waited for the results until one day, unexpectedly, Colonel Peake called me to announce that I had been selected for promotion. Finally! After twenty-four years in the Army, I was selected to the rank of colonel! When I was informed of my selection, I was so overcome with emotion that I let out a loud cheer. I called my family and some of my colleagues in the U.S. mainland to share the great news. They were all very happy.

There was total jubilation among the officers and non-commissioned officers in the hospital when they learned of my promotion. My Korean employees bowed respectfully as they extended their congratulations in broken English.

When the names of the selectees were released, I received multiple phone calls and letters congratulating me. General Louis C. Menetrey, who occupied several top leadership positions in South Korea, sent me a congratulatory letter. Though I'd never met him, most officers had heard of General Menetrey and understood his influence and importance in the Army. He wrote, "Congratulations on your promotion to colonel. This selection is truly an important milestone in your career and indicative of your potential for future increased professional responsibilities and challenges."[4]

Another—and perhaps the most significant—letter was from Brigadier General Bruce T. Miketinac, Chief of the Army Medical Service Corps. General Miketinac was a superb Army officer and someone I had looked up to throughout my military career. In his letter, General Miketinac stated, "Each member of the Medical Service Corps joins me in congratulating you on your recent selection for promotion to colonel. This selection was based on your demonstrated performance and is indicative of your potential to assume positions of increased responsibility in the Army and the Army Medical Department." Below his signature, General Miketinac wrote in his own handwriting: "Finally, the Army did something right. Way to go, Jake! M."[5]

When the promotion date arrived, Major General Frederick N. Bussey (who was visiting South Korea) and Colonel Peake "pinned" the new rank on my uniform. When Colonel Peake asked me to say a few words, I thanked everyone for attending the ceremony and highlighted the many sacrifices I had made to fulfill my career aspirations. I mentioned the dedication, tenacity, and hard work required to achieve the rank of colonel. I also encouraged those present, and especially the officers under my supervision, to never give up on their dreams and aspirations; to persevere and focus on being the best they could be.

Image 25. The author being promoted to colonel by Major General Frederick N. Bussey and Colonel James Peake

One of the most fulfilling experiences of my tour in Korea was serving as a preceptor to a Korean Catholic priest who was pursuing a degree in healthcare administration from the University of Minnesota. His name was Nicholas Chang, and he was the chief administrator of St. Mary's Hospital in Yeongdeungpo-gu, Seoul. When he learned that I held a master's degree (in the same field) from Baylor University, he visited my office to ask for my help.

We agreed to meet on Friday evenings to review the requirements of his studies. I also edited his papers, but it wasn't all about work. Father Chang was always happy and full of energy. He was so appreciative of my help that every so often would invite me to his home for dinner. Other times, he invited me to restaurants where only Koreans dined and introduced me to the most exotic dishes. He benefitted from our dinner meetings, but I also learned an awful lot about the Korean people, their culture, and their traditions from him.

On December 29, 1989, the University of Minnesota officially appointed me as Father Chang's preceptor and thanked me for my willingness to help him. Near the end of my tour, I invited him and his secretary to the 8th Army Officers' Club, an officers-only club. At the end of our dinner—and with teary eyes—he thanked me for my help and gave me a beautiful ceramic vase, which, after all these years, I still have.

RIFTS

Prior to my promotion to colonel, my wife and I had reached a standstill concerning our future together. My ambition was to remain in the Army and pursue my lifelong goal of becoming a colonel. In contrast, my wife no longer wished to continue her life as an Army wife and hoped I would choose to retire. Regrettably, I placed my own needs, desires, and ambitions above hers. This imbalance fostered resentment and weakened our emotional connection. As trust diminished, the distance between us grew and our relationship ultimately failed.

Life isn't always fair. I had achieved my long-term Army career goal, but unfortunately, my marriage was experiencing a rift. Before the end of my tour, I requested an assignment in San Antonio, Texas, to try and salvage the relationship.

I was assigned as the executive officer of the Department of Defense Combat Casualty Care Course. Known as C4, this eight-day program was designed to enhance the operational readiness and pre-deployment skills of tri-service (Army, Navy, and Air Force) medical officers. The C4 job was not the best one available, but I felt that being in San Antonio was best for me and my family. The most notable accomplishment of my tour of duty at C4 was its deployment to Chile. We transported our personnel and equipment, tailoring the C4 to the needs of the Chilean Army. Thanks to the support of Colonel Manuel Vitis Engelsberg, head of the Chilean medical forces, the training we provided was successful. We trained a large group of physicians, nurses, and ancillary personnel.

Unfortunately, my wife and I were unable to overcome our issues and decided to end our marriage. Sometimes the military can take a toll on one's marriage and differences cannot be reconciled. I felt sad, angry, and frustrated that my marriage had turned out this way. I also felt a significant loss—like the death of a loved one. I was grieving, anxious about the future, and venturing into the unknown.

After my one-year tour at C4, I was transferred to Fort Detrick, Maryland, for my last Army assignment as Deputy Chief of Staff for Operations (DCSOPS) of the U.S. Army Medical Research and Development Command (USAMRDC). Being assigned to Fort Detrick was not the assignment I wanted, but I was committed to make the best of it and give it my all. As DCSOPS, I managed several overseas laboratories in Brazil, Thailand, and Europe. I also managed the security and military intelligence functions at our headquarters. Having no experience with Army research, I knew this job would open the door to this fascinating military field. I also knew that this was my last assignment, and I would have to begin planning my transition from the Army.

As part of my job, I visited various laboratories at Army bases around the U.S. I also planned a military research conference in Israel. During a visit to the Fort Detrick Education Center, I learned of a PhD program in education sponsored by Walden University. A former Baylor program classmate, Lieutenant Colonel Glenn Makela, was one of its students. I already held a postgraduate degree in healthcare administration, as well as having ample experience managing healthcare organizations. Nevertheless, I believed I could leverage a PhD to find a college job if I couldn't find one in healthcare after retirement. I applied to the program and was accepted. During my last two years in the Army, I dedicated myself to my studies during the evenings and weekends.

RETIREMENT

After two years at Fort Detrick, on May 27, 1993, I retired from military duty at Fort Myer, Virginia. My mother, my oldest brother, and my sister-in-law flew in from Puerto Rico to celebrate with me. My daughter also flew in from Texas. Major General Fred A. Gorden, commander of the Military District of Washington, hosted the retirement ceremonies. They included an impressive parade, precision marching, speeches, and the presentation of retirement certificates.

The 3rd U.S. Infantry Regiment (traditionally known as the "Old Guard"), the U.S. Army Band, and the Fife and Drum Corps participated. [The regiment conducts memorial affairs to honor fallen comrades, ceremonies and special events, including sentinels of the Tomb of the Unknown Soldier. The Fife and Drum Corps recalls the days of the American Revolution as they perform in uniforms patterned after those worn by the musicians of General George Washington's Continental Army.]

I knew General Gorden from my assignment at Fort Ord where he was the assistant commander of the 7th Infantry Division. Because he was fluent in Spanish, he congratulated me in my native tongue. As the Soldiers marched in front of me, I reminisced about the many challenges I had faced and my accomplishments since my entry into active duty in 1968. I felt a mix of emotions, including pride, gratitude, and excitement.

I didn't have time to relax because, the following day, I was awarded the Legion of Merit (a U.S. military award, typically reserved for senior officers at colonel level and above, for exceptionally meritorious conduct, outstanding service, loyalty, and fidelity)—and the Medical Service Corps Medallion—at a retirement luncheon at Fort Detrick. After the medal was awarded, I called my mom to the front, removed the Legion of Merit medal from my chest, and—with misty-eyed reverence—pinned it on her. It was the best way I could find to recognize her for all the sacrifices she had made on my behalf and for the great influence she had on me.

Image 26. The author pinning his Legion of Merit medal on his mom during his retirement ceremony

My retirement marked the end of a successful and exciting career. After twenty-seven years of honorable military service, I looked forward, with a mix of anxiety and enthusiasm, to transitioning into the private sector.

Image 27. Major General (Retired) Enrique Méndez, Jr. and Major General Richard T. Travis officiate the author's retirement from active duty

CHAPTER 6

TRANSITIONING INTO THE PRIVATE SECTOR

FOR SEVERAL YEARS BEFORE MY RETIREMENT, I CONSIDERED three options for post-military work: private sector management consultant, civilian work in the military, or higher education.

As a healthcare management consultant in the private sector, I could leverage my years of experience in the Army and my postgraduate degree in healthcare management to get a challenging job with better pay. As a civilian employee in the military healthcare system, I'd be working in the same system I had retired from—continuing my previous life—which would not have been challenging enough for me. Job opportunities in higher education appealed to me; they were my second choice after management consultant. Private healthcare consulting presented an unknown, exciting, and unexplored terrain. A fallback alternative within the healthcare field was to work as a healthcare administrator in the private sector.

While in the Army, I had been preparing for a private sector job and remained up to date in the healthcare management field, expanded my professional network, and attended multiple workshops about transitioning from the military. I also continued to learn about healthcare challenges, always maintained an updated resume, and enrolled in courses on interviewing and how to dress for success in the private sector.

Six months before my retirement, I learned about a hospital chief executive officer (CEO) job opening in Ecuador. Although not a healthcare consultant job, the opportunity to manage a hospital for a mining company seemed interesting. In addition, the hospital CEO had to establish a program to train the hospital staff and emergency medical technicians. My years of military training and healthcare administration gave me the confidence to apply. I forwarded my resume to the search committee and received a reply by email almost immediately. They asked for my phone number.

The search committee had considerable interest in interviewing me. Three days later, the head of the search committee called. I had been ill with the flu for a couple of days, but I answered it anyway. Being sick precluded me from being at my best—I only wanted to finish the conversation and rest. The following day, I realized that I had made a serious mistake by allowing an interview by telephone when I was not feeling well. I should have asked for a face-to-face on-site interview. I did not hear back from the search committee, but the interview was a good training experience.

A month later, I learned that a global consulting firm in Northern Virginia was looking for a bilingual executive with healthcare management experience. The firm wanted to establish a consulting team focused on Latin America. The team would market, sell, and manage healthcare management projects in the region. The job seemed like a great opportunity. It would allow me to leverage my healthcare experience and my biculturalism. I forwarded my resume and was immediately contacted by the executive search firm. The interviewer mentioned that the job was in Caracas, Venezuela. I did not want to move to Venezuela but applied anyway, hoping that this requirement could be negotiated.

The hiring firm invited me to travel to Venezuela with a vice president of the consulting firm as part of the interview process. The vice president would be the future supervisor of the selected candidate. During our flight, we discussed several aspects of the job and my experience. When I inquired about the purpose of the trip, he said, "Jake, we are going to evaluate a public hospital in Caracas." When I asked how we should split our roles and which areas I should evaluate, he replied, "I am not a healthcare expert—I am going there to observe." That's when I realized the real purpose of the trip was to evaluate me and how well I knew hospitals and healthcare management.

We arrived the day before the hospital evaluation. The following morning, a car waited at our hotel to take us to the hospital. The driver asked me, in Spanish, if I was sure we wanted to go to the Catia neighborhood. After checking my notes, I confirmed that the hospital in Catia was the one we needed to visit. As we approached it, I could tell it was not the safest of environments. Trash was piled up on the sidewalks and the buildings were run-down and faded.

My traveling companion had never traveled to Latin America and didn't speak Spanish. As we approached the hospital, he whispered to me, "Jake, I don't feel comfortable being in these surroundings."

Trying to reassure him, I said, "Don't worry. Venezuelans are very hospitable; everything is going to be fine."

When we arrived at the hospital, the CEO warmly greeted us. I explained the purpose of our visit and the fact that this was our first visit to Caracas. When he asked if we had any questions, the vice president (in true consultant fashion) interjected, "Sir, can you share some of your major challenges?"

After I translated into Spanish, the CEO seriously said, "One of our main challenges is that patients commit crimes against the staff."

The vice president's eyes opened wide. "Sir, what do you mean?"

The CEO continued, "Some patients steal hospital equipment, and yesterday one of them robbed and stabbed a surgeon."

When asked how this could be possible, the CEO said, "The surgeon asked the patient why he had done such a horrible thing, after saving his life, and he casually replied, "Your job is to save lives—mine is to rob people!"

The vice president gasped, unable to hide his fear.

After first inspecting the hospital's safety procedures, supplies, and medical records, I visited the human resources office. The hospital had more employees on the payroll than were showing up for work. Many retired employees stayed on the payroll because it was cheaper than paying their retirement pay plus all their accrued benefits. I was dumbfounded by the situation—the hospital was worse than I thought possible! After finishing the evaluation, I presented my observations to the CEO and told him that I would put them in writing with recommended actions for improvement.

Before saying our farewells, I inquired about a taxicab to take us to the hotel. The CEO replied that taxicabs did not operate after 3 p.m. because the neighborhood was extremely unsafe. After much scrambling and phone calling, he found an employee from custodial services willing to take us.

When we saw the employee's car, our hearts sank! It was very old, dilapidated, and in need of repair. It was a very hot day, so I asked the VP to sit in the front seat so he could enjoy the view of the city and the tiny flow of lukewarm air blowing from the air-conditioning system. As we drove through the neighborhood, we saw just as much trash as we had seen before. Suddenly, we hit a pothole, and the car's radio fell onto the VP's lap! A few minutes later, sweating profusely because of the intense tropical heat and with the car's radio still on his lap, we arrived at our hotel.

On the flight back to the States, the vice president mentioned that I would be a great addition to their consulting team. I asked for additional information about the firm, and he stated that it was divided into private sector and government client groups. When I inquired about the difference between them, he smiled and sarcastically said, "Jake, consultants for private sector clients travel first class and drink wine. Government sector consultants travel on coach and drink beer." I asked in which client group I was going to be employed (if hired). He immediately said, "The private sector."

I returned his mischievous smile and replied, "That sounds good to me!"

THE SALARY QUESTION

Suddenly, the tone of his voice changed. Looking at me seriously, he said, "Jake, we need to talk about salary—what type of compensation are you looking for?"

I had anticipated the salary question but didn't realize it was going to come so soon. I had learned, during career transition workshops, not to make a salary commitment early in the interview process. It was more important to determine if the job was a good fit. I demurred, stating that I needed additional time to think about it. The salary question was difficult to answer. In my twenty-seven years of military service, I had never had to negotiate my salary. My military compensation was based primarily on my rank and how long I had been in the Army.

After our trip, I received several calls from the firm's Human Resources Office asking for my decision about joining their consulting team. They also wanted an answer to the salary question, but the requirement to move overseas did not appeal to me. I was at my wits' end when, at a workshop for my PhD studies, I met a classmate who needed help writing a term paper. I volunteered to help him. He was so appreciative that he invited me to lunch. During lunch, I informed him that I was getting ready to transition into the private sector. When I mentioned that I was "stuck" on the salary question, his eyes lit up. He said, "Jake, you have been very kind helping me and I want to help you too. I work as a consultant, advising executives with their compensation packages. I'll call you tonight and we can discuss the issue further."

Around 7 p.m., I reviewed the job offer with him, as well as the requirement to move to Venezuela. I told him that I wanted the job but did not want to move overseas.

After listening carefully, he replied, "Jake, make a list of the following relocation costs: transporting your household goods to Venezuela; renting an executive apartment; hiring a driver and maid; trips to Puerto Rico and Texas to visit your family; one trip a year for your children to visit you; office rental and secretary." The list was quite long and costly. He continued, "Call the Human Resources Office and inform them of the costs they would incur if you relocated. Then, offer them the alternative of working from their offices in Northern Virginia or your home in Maryland and traveling, as needed, to Latin America."

When I presented the list, the firm was shocked by the relocation and on-site costs and was amenable to me working from Northern Virginia. They also proposed a good salary, which I promptly accepted. A month later, I began the next phase of my professional career as a private sector consultant!

MUCH TO LEARN

Prior to my first day of work, following Army tradition, I wrote a letter to my supervisor asking to have workspace reserved for me. When I arrived, I asked his secretary for directions to my office and she gave me a blank stare. I asked, again, if she had office space available for me and she suggested that I look around for unoccupied space.

After wandering around for a few minutes, all I could find was a small office with some unused, dust-covered furniture. I went back to the secretary, gave her the location of my newly found space, and asked for any written procedures that would help me understand the consulting organization. She gave me a quizzical look and indicated that they didn't have written procedures, but she did give me two numerical codes: one to use the telephone in my office and one for the copy machine. She also informed me I would be getting a corporate credit card and a calling card to make long-distance phone calls.

I never had credit cards or numerical codes in the military and, prior to one's arrival, everything was done to make a newcomer comfortable. The company's welcome left me confused and nervous. When I asked about my boss, I learned that he worked remotely from his home in Mississippi. I had always worked as a member of a team at the same location. Not having my supervisor nearby was totally unexpected. I was worried because I wouldn't have someone nearby to turn to, but working independently also gave me a sense of relief at not having to answer to someone all the time. I realized that I had much to learn about my new work environment.

I went back to my office, and the telephone rang as soon as I sat down. My boss gave me my first assignment: to travel to Atlanta and help him hire new members for our consulting team. Unsure what to do, I went back to the secretary, who taught me how to arrange air travel and make hotel reservations. I felt unprepared for this assignment but hoped that my boss would share details about the hiring process in Atlanta.

On my first morning in Atlanta, I had an early breakfast with my boss. I'd never had to interview or hire candidates in the Army because the military personnel system selected and assigned Soldiers. I asked him for some tips on selecting candidates. His advice was simple. "Jake, hiring is not difficult. You review the candidate's resume and, after conducting an interview, determine if the individual is qualified. Next, if you believe you can travel with him or her for two consecutive weeks, that person is a good hire." I have never forgotten that advice. It iterated something I already knew, that being personable and getting along with others was key to any job.

I adjusted well to this new role. One of the first candidates I interviewed was a young physician and graduate of a prestigious university in Chicago. He was bilingual, very intelligent, and knew healthcare management. After interviewing him, I concluded that he was an excellent candidate and should be hired. I informed my boss of the results of the interview and, a couple of weeks later, he was asked to join our team. Hiring him was a good decision because he became a great asset to all of us.

DEVELOPING TRUST

I knew that developing business opportunities for healthcare consulting in Latin America was going to be difficult. It would take considerable time to develop trust and confidence with prospective clients (healthcare executives and government officials in the region). U.S. executives did not understand that; they expected those we visited to buy our services right away based on the reputation and capabilities of the firm we represented.

Healthcare administration was not a recognized profession in Latin America, leaving administration in the hands of untrained individuals. Because of that, their hospitals lacked modern management systems to improve efficiency, enhance patient care, and reduce costs. Our goal was to show them how to restructure how they ran their hospitals to make them more efficient, adopt new approaches to improve patient care, and make them cost-effective.

I also visited the World Bank and the Inter-American Development Bank to learn about previous loans approved for healthcare projects in the region. Studying these projects would help us identify consulting opportunities and tailor the restructuring methodologies to be used. To develop trust, we offered free evaluations and proposals to healthcare organizations. Those proposals laid out the hospital's weaknesses, explained how we could help them, and provided bank information to show them how they could afford our services.

Local governments managed many hospitals, but working with them was also a challenge. When I shared my one-week consulting fee with the health minister of Ecuador, his eyes widened—it was the same as his month's salary. I learned then that it was going to be difficult to sell proposals to the governments.

Working in Colombia

Consultants in our firm stayed at nice hotels, but when we sold our first project in Bogotá, Colombia, I felt that my team would be more efficient if we rented an apartment and stayed together. Plus, it reduced the cost of the project. Besides managing the program, I had to evaluate several areas of the hospital and market our services to prospective clients.

I remember vividly what my vice president said during our trip to Venezuela. "Jake, in this business, we work projects for eight hours, market our firm for four hours, and write proposals for four hours every workday." Our days were long, but I enjoyed the work tremendously. Sharing my knowledge for improving hospital operations was fulfilling. It was also exciting to work in such a beautiful country while leveraging my bilingual abilities and the expertise of my team.

While working on the project, I neared the end of my PhD studies and needed to defend my doctoral thesis. I could not abandon the project to travel to the U.S. to do so in person, so I contacted the university to propose a conference call. Initially, the university balked. Their academic rules called for face-to-face interaction between students and dissertation committees. After explaining my reason for being in Colombia, however, the university agreed, but I had to coordinate with my dissertation committee and provide the university with a typed transcript of the call.

There was no Skype, Zoom, or similar technology in 1994. The burden was on me to figure out how the conference call was going to be held. I went to work immediately by researching firms dedicated to providing international conference call services and, after much research, found a firm that did this and also recorded and typed written transcripts of telephone calls. In addition, an operator organized the call and reached out to all participants. I only had to provide their location, names, and phone numbers, as well as the date and time I wanted the call initiated.

After coordinating with members of my dissertation committee and selecting a date, I spent considerable time preparing to defend my thesis. The CEO offered me his office, and on the agreed-upon date and time, I waited patiently for the call. Right on cue, the phone rang, and I was in clear communication with my dissertation committee.

The two-hour call went flawlessly. I felt a great sense of relief but had to wait to hear back from the committee. When the CEO learned I had successfully defended my thesis, he hosted a special lunch to celebrate. My colleagues and the hospital staff were in awe. They could not believe that I was able to coordinate an international conference call with transcription support with three people, in three different time zones, for such a long period of time!

Several months after completing the Colombia project, the CEO informed me that the hospital won an award for innovation for the restructuring work we did. The award was going to be presented at a conference in the city of Medellín. He asked me to attend and give a presentation about our project. I had never visited Medellín but had learned that it was a beautiful city.

I landed at the Medellín airport late at night. After gathering my luggage and undergoing the customs inspection, I hailed a taxicab. As we traveled along some winding and dark back roads, the driver turned around and nonchalantly asked, "Doctor (a term commonly used in Colombia to show respect), are you going to feel safe in Medellín?"

I responded, "Of course, why do you ask?"

"Well," the driver continued, "the hotel you are staying at was one of Pablo Escobar's favorites."

The presentation went well. As I stepped down from the stage, the CEO thanked me for the work our team had performed. I was pleased with the quality of our work and the experience I had acquired during my first consulting project. It was very challenging to be project manager and consultant at the same time, but the outcomes we achieved were well worth the sacrifice and hard work.

My team was still marketing our consulting capabilities in Latin America when I learned our firm was no longer pursuing healthcare projects in the region. This news devastated the team. We were making progress in the area and had potential projects we thought we could sell. Working in Latin America was the reason I had joined the firm, so I started seeking work elsewhere.

MANAGING KNOWLEDGE

I was making plans to visit my mom when a former colleague of mine called. He wanted to know if I was interested in joining the Government Consulting Services (GCS) at Electronic Data Systems (EDS). EDS provided information technology services to federal agencies: the Immigration and Naturalization Service, the Department of Defense healthcare delivery system, the Central Intelligence Agency, the Department of Veterans Affairs, and the Federal Emergency Management Agency. GCS needed an expert in the healthcare sector of the Department of Defense (DOD). I knew the DOD healthcare system well, so I sent him my resume. After a couple of interviews, I was hired as a managing consultant.

When I arrived, I focused my efforts on two sectors: the U.S. Army Medical Department and Latin America, but my focus expanded into Knowledge Management and Distance Learning (e-learning), new disciplines with considerable potential for growth. Knowledge Management interested me because during my military career, I saw the need to capture and share the expertise of medical personnel prior to their retirement. I always marveled at how many "new projects" in military medicine had, in fact, been tried before.

To help government agencies understand how we could help them, I visited several agencies, including the Department of Veterans Affairs Central Office (VACO), the U.S. Navy Bureau of Medicine and Surgery, and the U.S. Army Medical Department Center and School (AMEDDC&S). During these visits, I gathered information about the organizations and gave a PowerPoint presentation about knowledge management. I also listed our consulting capabilities.

At that time, Major General James Peake, my former boss in Korea, was the head of the Army Medical Department Center and School (AMEDDC&S) in San Antonio, Texas. Like me, he was concerned about the loss of intellectual capital. I suggested a knowledge management presentation for his senior team, and he agreed. Two weeks later, we gave our presentation. It was well received, but then the hard work of preparing a proposal and selling the project began!

The AMEDDC&S had established a Center for Healthcare Education and Studies (CHES) that was led by a former Army colleague who had attended our presentation. Meeting with him, I iterated the benefits that knowledge management could bring to the CHES and the Army Medical Department, and he agreed. I suggested that he assign an officer with whom I could coordinate the development of a proposal. He appointed one of his most trusted officers as his lead, someone I had worked with at the HSC Headquarters eight years earlier.

When I visited her, we resumed our former collegial relationship. She knew the basic principles of knowledge management and its potential. That was good news; I did not have to spend additional time going over my prepared presentation. She was interested in receiving our proposal but was concerned about the cost. I shared her concern; I knew that the organization didn't have a tremendous amount of money in its budget. When I returned to my office, I feverishly worked on a reasonable proposal. I knew the project would take considerable time and effort but chose to develop a proposal for a first phase only to make it more appealing.

I obtained GCS approval for the proposal and the green light to deliver it to the client. When I delivered it, I learned that our cost estimate came very close to the funding she had allocated in her budget. After a few minor changes to the project plan, we agreed on a starting date. This was an exciting day for GCS— we had sold our first knowledge management project! For me, it was doubly exciting because the project, known thereafter as the Knowledge Management Network (KMN), was in support of the Army Medical Department, an organization to which I had dedicated twenty-seven years of selfless service.

The GCS director asked if I wanted to be the KMN's program manager. I respectfully declined his offer. It would have required me to move to San Antonio, something not appealing to me. I enjoyed being a managing consultant much more than managing projects on site. However, I was so invested in the project that I traveled to San Antonio once a month to support the AMEDDC&S. As the months went by, the KMN grew into a three-year engagement. I was overjoyed by the outcome—our first knowledge management project was a success.

ARGENTINA

Because of my continued interest in Latin America, I attended conferences focusing on the region to explore potential opportunities. During one conference in San Diego, I met an entrepreneur who was looking to develop business partnerships in the U.S. to provide training in Argentina.

His name was Oscar, and we connected instantly. My commitment to the region impressed him, and he promised to reconnect after his return to Buenos Aires. A week later, he called to inform me that he was traveling to Washington, DC and would like to see me.

Oscar always carried two cell phones and a pocket full of batteries to replace those which had lost power. He was constantly on the phone. During our first lunch, he ordered a grilled cheese sandwich with a tall glass of whole milk. He suffered from stomach ulcers and survived, mainly, on this meal. During one of our meetings over his now familiar sandwich, he shared his vision to engage a reputable U.S. university to train Argentine government officials. The opportunity interested me because these officials could help us identify consulting opportunities in Argentina. I promised to get back to him.

I had a friend at George Washington University who had developed a training program with me during the previous year for Argentine healthcare executives. The program had been successful; we trained over 100 executives in Washington, DC, and Argentina. I told him about Oscar's plan, and my friend agreed that we could modify our program for Oscar's needs. We planned a trip to Argentina to meet with him and his partners to discuss the opportunity. Two months later, we sold our training program.

As co-leader of the project, I traveled and lectured extensively throughout Argentina to show our expertise in healthcare management. I visited fascinating locations, including the beautiful city of Salta with its elegant, cafe-lined public square; Jujuy Province, the gateway to Argentina's indigenous heartland bordering Bolivia and Chile; and Ushuaia, the southernmost city in the world. Traveling was cumbersome. Oftentimes I had to return to Buenos Aires to make connections because there were no direct flights between cities. Besides my work in Argentina, I also supported the KMN project in San Antonio. My traveling schedule was extremely busy.

After the conclusion of our project in Argentina, I marketed and sold two e-learning projects for which I also served as project manager. One of the projects involved the development of an e-learning strategic plan for a public university in Puerto Rico.

HIDDEN AGENDAS

A new aspect of private sector life that I learned to navigate was hidden agendas. During the project in Puerto Rico, our agendas and project plan often collided with the group's discussions and arguments. Quite often, I acted as a referee to settle disputes among members of the team.

There was a huge personal bonus to our project though. It took place thirty-five minutes from my mom's home, giving me the unique opportunity to visit her often. Walking down her sidewalk and smelling the nutty and smoky aroma of the delicious Puerto Rican coffee she always prepared was a special treat. When I stayed with her overnight, I slept in my old bed, listening to nature's tropical sounds, which returned me to the wonderful years of my childhood.

Despite its challenges, I enjoyed my private sector career. The personal sacrifices (long work hours, constant travel, and adjusting to a new work environment and clients) had been significant, but the rewards had been worth the effort. I had traveled extensively throughout the continental U.S., Latin America, Europe, and Australia, accumulating over one million air miles. Most importantly, I successfully transitioned out of the military. Comfortable in my new role, I expected to end my career in the private sector.

CHAPTER 7

AT THE WEST WING OF THE WHITE HOUSE

THE METRO TRAIN'S WHEELS SQUEAKED WITH A LOUD HISSING and screeching noise as it slowed to a stop in the McPherson Square Metro Station, a quarter mile from the White House. After the customary loudspeaker warning, the doors opened wide. I stepped onto the platform and walked briskly until I exited onto Vermont Avenue, turning right past the Department of Veterans Affairs Central Offices (VACO). Little did I know that I was going to occupy a presidentially appointed senior position at the VACO in three months.

Ten minutes later, I arrived at the Northeast Gate of the White House and showed the guard my driver's license. I told him I had an appointment in the Office of Presidential Personnel. I couldn't believe I was saying those words!

The guard issued me a pass—attached to a chain to be worn around my neck—and asked me to proceed to the right side of the White House into its West Wing. As I proceeded, I noticed a group of news media reporters with their equipment at the ready. A sharp-looking U.S. Marine, in his impeccable uniform, stood by the building's entrance. As I approached, the Marine grabbed the door handle and opened the door.

At the Office of Presidential Personnel, an assistant greeted me. As I shook his hand, he looked at me intently and, with a slight Texas accent, said, "Dr. Lozada, welcome to the Office of Presidential Personnel. Your name has been mentioned as a potential candidate for a job in President Bush's administration. We wanted to meet you and talk to you about it."

Startled by that introduction, I could only reply, "Thank you, sir. It would be a great honor and privilege to work for the president of the United States."

He asked me to sit down by his desk and as I sat, said, "Please tell me about yourself." After I finished sharing the highlights of my life story, he stood and said, "Guys, come and meet Dr. Jacob Lozada, a great example of the American Dream."

I was taken aback by his statement. Pushing myself to find the right words and glancing quickly at his eyes, I said, "Sir, I am only someone from humble beginnings who has worked very hard and succeeded against many odds. I owe it mostly to hard work, my wonderful parents, and the opportunities our great nation has given me." Although I considered myself a good example of the American Dream, I didn't expect him to mention it during the interview.

After I met several other people in the office, the assistant mentioned he was interested in interviewing other well-accomplished Hispanics for President Bush's Administration and asked how to find more people like me. I replied by stating that I would enjoy recommending friends and former colleagues I knew who met his criteria.

Prior to my interview, I had read about the presidential appointment process and was aware of the many questions which would be asked. The interviewer asked me multiple questions about my personal life, my professional careers in the Army and private sector, and my motivation to serve the president of the United States. He also asked me to disclose any issues that might embarrass the president if he chose to nominate me. After answering a barrage of questions, the conversation turned to which jobs in President Bush's administration best matched my professional profile and would be of interest to me.

With my military background and healthcare experience, two departments immediately came to mind: the Department of Defense and the VA. I had a very good understanding of healthcare within DOD as well as service members' issues. As a veteran, I understood the challenges the VA and our veterans faced and believed I could help fix some of them. The interviewer next asked which jobs at the VA I felt most suited for. I mentioned two: Assistant Secretary for Management and Assistant Secretary for Human Resources and Administration. For the Department of Defense, I mentioned a senior position in military medicine. After a lengthy discussion, we agreed that a senior position at the VA was the best fit for me.

When I inquired about the next steps, the interviewer told me that a senior position at the VA would need Senate confirmation. I would undergo several investigations, and the results would be reviewed by offices in the White House, the United States Senate, and the VA. These organizations would also review my financial, medical, and other personal information. I was also warned that it was difficult to predict when I would know more about my nomination since many other candidates were also being considered. Bottom line, the process could be lengthy and frustrating. Until then, the Office of Counsel to the President would interview me the next day. Before leaving his office, I was instructed not to disclose my interview with anyone.

Despite my agreement not to talk about the interview, after I exited the Office of Presidential Personnel I couldn't contain my excitement. I stopped in a corner of the lobby and called my mom. She could not believe I was at the White House and was even more surprised when I told her that I was being interviewed for a job in President Bush's administration. Speaking in a gentler tone, she said, "Jacob, I don't want you to be disappointed if you don't get the job—just being interviewed at the White House makes me, our hometown, and Puerto Rico proud."

The following morning, I reported to the Office of Counsel to the President. Unlike my previous interview, this office buzzed with activity. A few seconds after being shown to an empty desk, a well-dressed, unsmiling man sat down and asked me, "Why do you want to serve the president of the United States?"

Without hesitation, I said, "Representing our nation's veterans, the Hispanic community in the mainland, and the people of Puerto Rico at the highest levels of government would be a tremendous personal accomplishment. It would also be a great opportunity to make a positive impact."

Without skipping a beat, he continued, "Is there anything in your personal and professional life that could embarrass the president?"

I thought very hard and couldn't come up with such an instance. I replied, "Sir, I can't think of anything in my personal and professional life that could embarrass the president."

He followed up with a series of rapid-fire questions about my beginnings in Puerto Rico, my personal life, and my professional careers. At times, it was difficult to stay focused and answer them quickly. After two hours of questions, I was almost worn out. I received a binder with information and multiple government forms to complete. Again, I was told not to divulge my White House interviews with anyone.

When I arrived home, I collapsed on the sofa and, sipping a glass of red wine, reviewed the binder. The forms were alien to me and cumbersome to complete. I had five days to fill out and return medical waivers, financial release forms, and consent forms, many of which required me to contact old friends in Puerto Rico and former colleagues on the mainland. I started working, knowing that even after I finished and submitted the paperwork, it would take time, maybe weeks, to find out if I got the job. If the president didn't nominate me, I would continue working at EDS. If he chose to nominate me, however, there would be several more steps. Below are the steps:

First, the president submits the nomination to the Senate. Then, the nomination is referred to the committee with jurisdiction over the position—in my case, Veterans Affairs—to conduct confirmation hearings to vet the candidate. After the hearings, the committee votes. If the nomination is approved, a vote is taken in the Senate to confirm or deny the nomination. Finally, once the nominee is confirmed by the Senate, the appointee takes the oath of office for his or her position.

Because I was not authorized to divulge that I was being considered for a position on President Bush's team, I had to figure out a reason for requesting the required information from old friends in Puerto Rico and former colleagues on the mainland without raising any suspicion. After some thought, I told them my private sector job required a renewed government security clearance. As part of that process, I had to provide a list of personal references with their contact information. I also warned them not to be concerned if they were approached by the FBI to provide additional information about me because it was all part of the security clearance renewal process.

A couple of days later, my home telephone rang. The caller identified herself as an FBI agent. With nerves on high alert, I politely asked, "How may I be of service to you?"

She stated, "I'm the agent assigned to your investigation, and I want to interview you as soon as possible." She gave me the choice of interviewing me at my home or a different place. I suggested we meet at a coffee shop in Falls Church, Virginia, twenty minutes from my home, the following morning. She agreed.

I left home early to allow for any traffic delays, arriving at 7:30 a.m. There was a high school near the coffee shop, and students were entering to purchase breakfast. I ordered a cup of coffee and sat near the counter. I must have become distracted because I did not notice a young woman, wearing a business suit, walking toward me. As she stopped by my table, she asked, "Are you Dr. Lozada?" After I answered yes, she reached into her purse and quickly showed her FBI identification. She continued, "I am an agent of the FBI, and I am here to interview you."

I leaped to my feet to shake hands and was taken aback by how young she was! She looked like any of the other high school students in the coffee shop; perhaps that was why I did not notice her approaching my table. She recommended that we move to a more secluded spot, away from the customers. I agreed.

When we took our new seats, she said, "I have several questions to ask, and some will be very personal. Is that okay with you?"

"That's fine, ma'am. I will answer all questions to the best of my knowledge and abilities."

She continued. "My questions are the beginning of a formal background investigation prior to being nominated for a senior position in the federal government. The investigation will also include interviews with individuals who've known you across many years." For the next hour, she bombarded me with multiple lightning-fast questions—from my early years in Puerto Rico to my recent work at EDS. Some of the questions were very personal in nature, others began with the phrase, "Have you ever . . .?" I was so glad we had moved away from other customers!

THE NEWS MEDIA

I was still completing the required forms when I received an unexpected telephone call from a reporter at the Puerto Rican newspaper *El Nuevo Día*. I was stunned! Other than my mom, I had not confided in anyone about my interviews. The reporter didn't waste any time. "Dr. Lozada, I am a reporter from *El Nuevo Día*. We have learned that you have been interviewed by the White House for a job in President Bush's administration."

Trying not to show my surprise, I replied, "I am very sorry, I can neither deny nor confirm that I was interviewed by the White House." Undeterred, she asked if I would call her when I was authorized to do so. I agreed, thinking that being open to the news media was a good practice.

The following day, I mentioned the reporter's call to my mom, and she chastised me for not helping the reporter. Concerned about the reporter losing her job for not completing her assignment, my mom made me promise to contact her as soon as I was authorized to do so.

MORE INTERVIEWS

As part of the nomination process, I had to interview with the VA transition team. One of its members knew the Senate very well and was familiar with Puerto Rico from visits he had made to the former Roosevelt Roads Naval Station. The second member had worked, for many years, in the Office of Legal Counsel at VACO. During the interview, they asked questions about my background, my motivation to occupy a senior position at the VA, and my knowledge of what lay ahead in the nomination process. They gave me tips for the Senate hearing, the protocol involved in answering questions, and which words to avoid.

The interviewers were down-to-earth and open, which helped me relax. The information they provided was invaluable—I was new to this environment and had never testified before the U.S. Congress. As the interview progressed, I became increasingly more comfortable and relaxed. As the conversation was ending, the lead interviewer abruptly stood up and said, "Dr. Lozada, let's go meet the secretary." Buoyed by the opportunity to meet the top leader at the VA, I quickly followed him into one of the main elevators.

On the 10th floor, we walked past several large photos on the wall. They depicted some of our veterans as well as some of our national cemeteries, including the one in Normandy, France. As I entered the secretary's office, I noticed a small window with a clear view of the White House. It was a beautiful sight! Across from his desk were several comfortable chairs arranged around a mahogany coffee table with a flower arrangement of red and white roses.

My escort introduced me. "Mr. Secretary, Dr. Jake Lozada is a retired Army colonel who works as a consultant in the private sector. He has been sent by the White House as a potential nominee for Assistant Secretary for Human Resources and Administration. We believe he will make a great addition to your team."

The secretary welcomed me. Inviting me to sit down, he asked, "Why do you want this job?" I said: "As a veteran with twenty-seven years of active military duty, there is no better job than serving my fellow veterans. Also, my experience in the private sector could be of value to the VA. President Bush has demonstrated great affinity toward the Hispanic community and representing them, at the top levels of the federal government, would be a great honor."

The secretary and I reviewed some of the challenges facing our nation's veterans and the VA. I listened attentively as he shared what I should expect during the Senate confirmation hearings. When I mentioned my consulting work in Latin America and my multiple trips to Argentina, he tilted his head and made steady eye contact. We discussed our experiences with Argentina, mine as a consultant and his as the birthplace of his father. I knew that his time was extremely valuable so, after exchanging a few more pleasantries, I asked to be excused. We shook hands again and, as I walked out of his office, he wished me the best of luck.

I asked my escort if he had any other questions or instructions for me. Upon hearing none, I quickly walked out and toward the Metro Station. The Orange Line train to Vienna came to a slow stop. I muscled my way in and began to reflect on the amazing events of the previous two days. I felt confident about my interview with the VA's transition team and my impromptu visit with the secretary. The unplanned meeting suggested I had made a good impression. That bolstered my confidence. I felt more confident about where I stood, thus far, in the nomination process.

WAITING IS HARD!

The coming days stretched on endlessly, my nerves on edge at the sound of my telephone ringing. While I waited to hear back from either the Office of Presidential Personnel or the VA's transition team, I attended an event sponsored by the National Association for Equal Opportunity in Higher Education (NAFEO). At lunch, I struck up a conversation with another Puerto Rican. During our conversation, I highlighted my travels in Latin America and my passion for mentoring and motivating Hispanic youth. Much to my surprise, he occupied a senior position in the VA's human resources organization and was awaiting word on who his next boss would be.

I chuckled inside. I was still bound by the White House directive not to reveal that I had been interviewed for the top position in human resources at the VA so, with the sincerest face I could muster, I said, "Don't worry. Things move slowly in the government. I'm sure you'll find out soon."

Finishing his lunch, he shook my hand and said, "Dr. Lozada, I enjoyed talking to you today. I admire your passion and energy as well as your commitment to our youth. I hope we can see each other again."

I returned his warm handshake and compliment by adding, "You should also feel proud of the work you do at VA and your commitment to our community. I am confident we will see each other again soon."

On Monday, April 25, 2001, the U.S. Newswire announced my nomination by the president as Assistant Secretary of Veterans Affairs for Human Resources and Administration.[1] I was allowed to grant interviews to the news media and immediately called the *El Nuevo Día* reporter. She was surprised by my call. I told her about the conversation I had with my mom. We both shared a good laugh. On May 2, 2001, *El Nuevo Día* also announced my nomination.[2] The article noted that I was from San Lorenzo but resided in Virginia.

I was not caught by surprise by the public announcements of my nomination. I had already been informed by the White House (before the nomination was made public) that the vetting process was going extremely well and the president intended to nominate me.

CHAPTER 8

MY SENATE CONFIRMATION HEARINGS

O N MAY 9, 2001, I RECEIVED A LETTER FROM THE U.S. Senate advising me that the Committee on Veterans Affairs had scheduled a hearing on my nomination. The letter invited me to testify at the committee's hearing to be held on May 16 at 9:30 a.m. in Room SR-418 of the Russell Senate Building.[1] Two days later, on May 11, I was brought into the VACO as an advisor/counselor. The White House allowed department and agency heads to bring potential future appointees into their organizations as advisors or counselors to the secretary.[2] I was pleased to receive a private office at the VACO as it enabled me to better prepare for the Senate confirmation hearings while I worked.

The Senate confirmation hearings required a tremendous amount of preparation. I had to review and memorize an incredible amount of information for them. I was pleasantly surprised by the warm welcome from the employees and their willingness to help me prepare. They provided me with everything I needed— internal documents, policies, and organizational charts. They also researched issues for me and obtained additional information for my review. Their support and commitment to my success during the hearings were a true testament to their non-partisan approach toward incoming senior political appointees. For that and all the courtesies extended to me, I will always be grateful.

During that time, I continued to be coached by the members of the VA Transition Office. They reviewed some of the questions the Senate committee might ask and stressed the importance of answering senators with, "If I were to be confirmed" or, "If I am honored with your confirmation" as a sign of deference. I needed to provide 100 copies of my testimony to the committee at least forty-eight hours prior to the hearing. Because there were five nominees (including me), I had to limit my oral statement to three minutes.

I also received a memorandum from the Deputy Assistant to the President for Legislative Affairs-Senate congratulating me on my selection by President Bush to be Assistant Secretary of Veterans Affairs for Human Resources and Administration. The memorandum included more paperwork: an explanation of the Senate confirmation process, instructions on how to proceed, and biographies of the senators serving on the committee.[3]

I worked in a frenzy to complete the forms given to me by the FBI and the Office of Ethics—they had to be finalized as soon as possible and returned to the White House Counsel's Office. The FBI's and the Office of Ethics' investigation would take thirty to forty-five days, so they encouraged me to schedule courtesy visits with members of the U.S. Senate Committee on Veterans Affairs. I immediately got to work filling out forms and making appointments.

GETTING INTO MY COMFORT ZONE

Though not required, I requested a visit to the Russell Senate Office Building to familiarize myself with the hearing room so I could get into my "comfort zone" during the hearing. As I entered the room, I noticed a large witness table and chair in the center. Three light bulbs (green, amber, and red) were on the table. The green light meant the witness had five minutes to speak, amber meant there was only one minute left, and red meant the witness needed to conclude their answer.

Behind the table were several rows of chairs facing the senators. I asked my escort which members of the committee would be in attendance, where they would sit, and who else would be in the room. I learned that representatives from the Veterans Service Organizations (VSOs), VACO staff, and congressional staff members would be there, and I could invite two guests.

I sat at the witness table, closed my eyes, and tried to visualize being in front of the senators, giving my opening statement, and answering their questions. When I opened my eyes, I looked behind me at the empty chairs and tried to visualize guests sitting behind me. After spending fifteen to twenty minutes familiarizing myself with the room, I departed with my shoulders back, chest out, and chin lifted— I felt confident.

Answering the Senators' Questions

On May 16, the four other VA candidates and I reported to the Russell Senate Office Building for the hearing. We walked into the room together, but before I took my seat in the front row, I surveyed my surroundings and greeted a few members of the audience. At 2:30 p.m., the committee chairman, Senator Specter, from Pennsylvania, in his customary booming voice, opened the hearing by noting that it was being held on an expedited basis due to the importance of confirming the VA's officers. Next, he called the five witnesses, one at a time.

When my turn came, I moved to the witness table. Those few steps seemed to take minutes instead of seconds. I looked behind me at the audience and saw some familiar faces smiling and beaming. As I faced the intimidating green, amber, and red lights, a sense of peace came over me. I slipped into my comfort zone and my nerves settled.

Chairman Specter asked me to stand up and raise my right hand to be sworn in. After this ceremonial procedure, I read my three-minute statement.

"Chairman Specter, Senator Rockefeller, and members of the committee, it is a great honor and privilege for me to appear before you today as President Bush's nominee for the position of Assistant Secretary for Human Resources and Administration of the Department of Veterans Affairs. Should I be confirmed, I will be deeply humbled by this opportunity to serve my country and our veterans, who have sacrificed for their country so valiantly. I would like to express my appreciation to the secretary of the VA for his support of my nomination to this position. I would also like to thank my family for their support throughout my entire professional career.

"The Department of Veterans Affairs faces many of the same human resources challenges which most government agencies face. These challenges result from an aging workforce, the competition for human resources in a prosperous economy, and the need for established organizations to transform themselves into lifelong learning organizations and high-performing enterprises. We can meet these challenges by working together and with the strong support and involvement of Congress, the Veterans Service Organizations, and our workforce representatives.

"We must focus our efforts on developing innovative human resource strategies that fully support the mission of the Department of Veterans Affairs, on improving the quality and access to service, and on supporting the strategic goals the secretary of the Department of Veterans Affairs has defined for the department.

"Human resources constitute the most important element of any organization. They are not a cost of doing business, but a valued asset that must be nurtured. The Department of Veterans Affairs can be a leader in hiring, developing, and maintaining a highly motivated human resources force. I want to be part of this exciting journey, and if confirmed, I promise to dedicate my efforts and apply my experience to achieve this vision.

"If I am honored with your confirmation, I will bring to this position twenty-seven years of experience as a commissioned officer and healthcare executive in the U.S. Army Medical Department, coupled with seven years as a consultant in large corporations in the private sector.

"During my military career, I had the opportunity to lead large organizations undergoing radical change; manage force structure, personnel allocations, and staffing; train and develop staff; and maintain high-performing teams. During my tenure in the private sector, I developed human resource programs for large organizations and led in the development of innovative training and knowledge management capabilities in support of human resource programs.

"Mr. Chairman, I would consider it an honor to work with you, other committee members, and your staff in meeting the human resource challenges of the Department of Veterans Affairs. It would be an honor to continue to serve our nation's veterans. I would be pleased to respond to any questions that you and other committee members may have. Thank you."[4]

Senator Rockefeller, from West Virginia, focused his questions on the relationship between VA and DOD. After assuring him of my intention to work toward win-win situations for both parties, he ended his questioning with, "It is just so important that we make the most of what we have, and I think you understand that very well. I look forward to working with you."[5]

As was his custom, Chairman Specter had a long list of follow-up questions. He asked that I submit my answers by the morning of May 21 (two working days after the hearing) and instructed each nominee to submit a report within sixty days outlining what we thought were the ten key issues facing VA.

When the hearing adjourned, I let out a sigh of relief and looked back at the audience. Those who knew me smiled. As

I exited the meeting room, shaking hands with my friends, members of the VA staff, and VSO representatives, many commented on how comfortable I looked and how quickly I answered the senators' questions. Their accolades humbled me. After a short reception for the candidates at the Army and Navy Club, I went home and started working on the questions from Senator Specter.

CONFIRMED UNANIMOUSLY!

I was checking and rechecking my emails when, on the morning of May 24, I received a short memo that the Senate Committee on Veterans Affairs would meet at three o'clock to report on my nomination. At 4 p.m., the VA secretary's office unexpectedly called to inform me that the senate had just confirmed me by a unanimous vote. I needed to report to the secretary's office immediately to be sworn in.

In the federal government, for an official to take office, he or she must first take the oath of office. I sprinted to the tenth floor and the secretary's office! When I arrived, the chief of staff and the general counsel of the VA were waiting for me. After the customary congratulations, the chief of staff produced a Bible and asked that I place my left hand on it while raising my right hand. The general counsel read the oath of office, and I repeated after him:

"I, Jacob Lozada, do solemnly swear that I will support and defend the Constitution of the United States against all enemies, foreign and domestic; that I will bear true faith and allegiance to the same; that I take this obligation freely, without any mental reservation or purpose of evasion; and that I will well and faithfully discharge the duties of the office on which I am about to enter. So help me God."

A warm glow of excitement expanded throughout my body after being sworn in. It ended a long, arduous—and at times frustrating—process. Becoming a presidential appointee was never in my career plans, but it was a true blessing and reward for my lifelong efforts to be all I could be. It was also an opportunity to be a role model and inspire others on a larger scale.

ISLAND PRIDE

News of my confirmation traveled fast. My mom called because the Office of the Governor of Puerto Rico had called to congratulate her on my appointment. I will never forget her exuberance! Getting the giggles, she said, "I am now a very important person, so you and your brothers better deal with me appropriately." After I reassured her that she was always the most important and respected person in our lives, we both laughed.

Several days later, I received a personal letter from the governor of Puerto Rico, extending her congratulations and asking that I extend the congratulations to my entire family. Of my appointment she said, "A triumph of a Puerto Rican fills those who had been born on that beloved island with tremendous pride."[6]

Several publications on the mainland, as well as the media in Puerto Rico, highlighted my confirmation and appointment. On Monday, June 4, the *El Nuevo Día* newspaper announced my Senate confirmation.[7] Many of my former colleagues and friends also expressed their congratulations.

One of the most touching and significant recognitions was a letter from my mom's church expressing the great pride and satisfaction they felt in having one of their sons, and a former member, appointed to such a prestigious position. Most members of my mom's church were humble people who had known me since my childhood. It was very touching to learn of their pride in my appointment to President Bush's leadership team. The letters of recognition and articles humbled me. When I read them, I experienced a mix of positive emotions, pride, and a sense of accomplishment. At the same time, I felt a slight embarrassment and awkwardness for being recognized in public.

CELEBRATION!

After my swearing in, I contacted the VACO's protocol office to help me plan a larger, more formal ceremony at the prestigious Army and Navy Club for my family, the VACO senior staff, and former colleagues. This was held on the morning of June 4, 2001. It began with the pledge of allegiance, the singing of the national anthem by a VACO employee, and the invocation by the director of the National Chaplain Service for the VA. My mom, my oldest brother and his wife, my daughter, and the mayor of my hometown traveled to Washington, DC, to attend the event. Their presence added a touch of home to the formal ceremony.

Major General Enrique Méndez spoke. He had been a mentor of mine and a friend for many years. He concluded by addressing my mom in Spanish:

> *"Doña Cuquín, Yo sé lo orgullosa que se siente usted hoy por el logro de su hijo. Pero también sé que ese logro es también suyo por los valores y la enseñanza que usted le inculcó a Jake y a sus otros hijos durante su formación. Yo conozco el inmenso cariño, respeto, y admiración que su hijo tiene por usted así que mi felicitación amiga y sincera de hoy va no solo a Jake sino en particular a usted, Doña Cuquín. ¡Bienvenida a Washington!"*

Translated: "Mrs. Cuquín (my mom's nickname), I know how proud you are today of your son's accomplishment. But I also know that this great accomplishment is also yours because of the values and teachings that you inculcated in Jake and your other sons during their formation. I know of the immense love, respect, and admiration that your son has for you, so my most friendly and sincere congratulations today are not only addressed to Jake but particularly to you. Doña Cuquín, welcome to Washington."

163

At the end of his kind remarks, there was not a dry eye in the room.

After Major General Méndez's remarks, the VA secretary administered the oath of office again. This time, my mom held her Bible for me. Having my mom at my swearing-in ceremony was an extraordinary experience.

Image 28. The author's mother holds her Bible as he is sworn in as Assistant Secretary for Human Resources and Administration

After the oath, it was a joy to shake hands with so many influential people from my past: Lieutenant General James Peake (Korea), Colonel (retired) Jack Danielson (Valley Forge General Hospital), and Lieutenant Colonel (retired) Glenn Makela (Fort Detrick), as well as personnel from the White House, staff members from the Puerto Rico Federal Affairs Administration (PRFAA), the mayor of San Lorenzo, several staffers from the U.S. Senate, and other VA political appointees.

Image 29. The author with his mom and daughter, Valerie, at the Army and Navy Club in Washington, D.C., during his formal swearing-in ceremony

After the festivities ended, I enjoyed the entire afternoon with my family. I had arranged tours of the White House and the Capitol, which my mom enjoyed the most. In the evening, we enjoyed a nice dinner in my home and recounted the day's events. The following morning, we had breakfast together before saying goodbye.

Then, it was time to get to work.

CHAPTER 9

SERVING THE PRESIDENT OF THE UNITED STATES

M Y NEW OFFICE WAS ON THE SECOND FLOOR OF THE VACO building, overlooking Lafayette Square and across from Pennsylvania Avenue and the White House. I supervised six organizations: the Human Resources Administration, Diversity and Equal Employment Opportunity, VACO Administration, Office of Security, Labor and Management Relations, and Office of Resolution Management.

Being a member of the president's subcabinet was a completely different environment. In the private sector, administrative support was scant. The senior leaders I knew there only had one administrative assistant. In my new role, however, my personal staff consisted of a Deputy Assistant Secretary (DAS), an executive assistant, and an administrative assistant. My DAS had many years of VA experience and knew practically everyone at the VACO. He acted on my behalf in my absence.

My executive assistant was a well-dressed young man who kept my calendar up to date. He coordinated my travel, proofread my speeches and presentations, and followed me everywhere to make sure I was on time for my appointments. He also oversaw the many administrative actions that arrived in my office for my approval. My administrative assistant was a gentle and easygoing woman. She took most telephone calls and worked closely with my executive assistant to complete administrative actions ahead of deadlines.

Soon after I assumed my new position, my office received multiple calls from Hispanic veterans and national Hispanic-serving organizations. As many of these callers only spoke Spanish and none of my assistants did, I was assigned yet another administrative assistant who was bilingual.

Obtaining feedback from my subordinates was always important to me, so every month I hosted a "Coffee with the Assistant Secretary." I purchased coffee and pastries, using my personal funds to avoid impropriety. One of my assistants randomly selected employees to attend. At these events, I encouraged employees to ask questions and share their concerns. From the start, these gatherings proved to be very useful. During the very first breakfast, I dispelled a rumor about a VA-wide reduction in force. I learned much about my employees from these breakfasts.

More Input

One day, I received an invitation from a former Army colleague who worked as a senior staffer in the U.S. Congress. We had not seen each other for over fifteen years, so it was exciting to reconnect. After we shared a few veterans' war stories, he congratulated me on my presidential appointment. He had considerable insights about the VA and quickly shared them. Although unsolicited, I listened actively to his ideas and appreciated his insights.

He had worked in Congress for several years and knew the VA issues very well. He listed some of VA's human resource challenges and strongly iterated something I already knew—that the system to award performance bonuses to top executives had been a source of considerable criticism. The VA, he said, "suffers from a pervasive culture of awarding good performance evaluations and cash bonuses to its executives. The performance evaluation system at the VA is broken—the executive bonuses given are not based on results." He also mentioned that the U.S. Congress was looking into the situation.

At the end of our conversation, I thanked him for his input. As I stood up to leave, he said, "Jake, let me give you a piece of advice. Don't trust anyone, I mean *anyone*."

I shook his hand and left his office.

As I traveled to the VACO, his words kept ringing in my head. I always believed in the goodness of people, and mistrust was not in my DNA.

BRIDGES AND PRIORITIES

An important part of my job was meeting with and receiving input from the Veteran Service Organizations. They were key stakeholders for veterans and could help me advance my priorities for addressing the human resource challenges at VA. Some former VSO staff members served at VA, providing a bridge between us and their organizations.

Image 30. The author with his son Jason at VACO— the White House in the background

I believed creating alliances with Hispanic organizations would benefit us all, so I invited several leaders to an introductory meeting. However, when I held my first meeting with leaders of these organizations, they made it clear that they knew the number of Hispanics working in the VA. They would not only be monitoring that number, but they would also use it as a standard to judge my performance.

Annoyed, but in a carefully controlled tone, I said, "Are you saying that you'll openly criticize me and denounce VA if I don't meet your quota of Hispanic employees? How does that help our Hispanic community? How does it help VA? And how does it help me support our nation's veterans?" These leaders did not understand that I had not been appointed to be an advocate for Hispanic issues.

Unfortunately, VA (like many organizations in the federal government) was an entrenched bureaucracy—difficult to change and slow to adjust to a rapidly changing world. To complicate matters, the department was constantly under surveillance by its many stakeholders, and career senior executives exerted a lot of influence and power. In the private sector, decision-making was quick, change was the "new normal," and organizational realignments were easy to implement. I promptly realized that to a fast-track leader like me, adjusting to the federal government culture was going to be challenging.

Being a change agent in the government was not easy. Every time a change was proposed, word traveled quickly, and the bureaucratic wagons circled around to delay, obfuscate, and often block the change. For some senior executives, their personal ambitions were more important than the organization's success. The resistance to change seemed to be stronger and quicker when the changes were suggested and ushered in by senior political appointees who were seen by some as "temporary help," as I was.

At one point, a member of my staff told me, "Dr. Lozada, executives in your position are only here for two to four years.

Our career executives will long outlive you. Why don't you just enjoy the perks of your position for the time being?"

INNOVATION

Despite his suggestion, and the prevailing opposition to innovation, I fought for change and introduced several innovative programs. One successful program was the VA Youth Council—an initiative in response to the challenge of an aging workforce and the government's struggle to attract young people. It brought a select group of young employees to the VACO to answer two questions: what brought them to the VA and what would make them stay? We used their ideas for marketing, recruiting, and establishing programs to improve employee retention. When their ideas launched, some of the older employees pushed back, but I supported these young employees' plans for addressing the challenge. Eventually, these older employees saw the benefit of listening to the younger employees who would eventually inherit the department.

Another program in need of innovation was the student internship program. This program introduced the department to young students. It also aimed at motivating students toward public service. Several internship programs existed at the VA, but with several flaws: they were expensive, they were not results driven (i.e., success was not based on students' demonstrated interest toward service at the VA), and they only targeted college students. I wondered if an internship program targeting younger students would yield better results.

I asked my diversity management staff to brainstorm a new internship program targeting high school students. They created the Summer Employment and Enrichment Program to launch in San Antonio in partnership with the Texas Workforce Commission. Unlike other student internships, this program targeted high school students and focused on developing one-on-one mentoring relationships, teaching life skills and positive routines, and motivating students to pursue job opportunities in the federal government. The curriculum included financial management, credit card debt, goal setting, and communication skills. We partnered with local schools to market the program, identify participants, and provide transportation. As a result, we were able to transport fifty-three students, ages sixteen to eighteen, from financially deprived families to program locations across Texas.

Most of these low-income Hispanics had limited chances of attending college or even completing high school. The internship prepared them to succeed at both. It also introduced them to careers in the federal government. All students completed the program. One attendee, talking in hushed, excited tones, said, "I gained so much experience working at the VA Hospital that my self-confidence really escalated. I see myself using work skills that I didn't even know I had."[1] At the graduation ceremony, parents beamed with pride as their children received their diplomas.

After the success of the internship program, my staff established a Student Career Academy in Baltimore, Maryland, in partnership with the Centers for Medicare and Medicaid Services and the Baltimore City Public Schools, for mentoring, job shadowing, and leadership development. The academy opened its doors in September 2002 to fifty disadvantaged and minority high school students. Each student was eligible for paid summer jobs in the federal government.

The unrelenting flow of tasks and deadlines at VA continued, and soon it was time again to select executives for performance bonuses. As I reflected on how to proceed, the criticism of VA's executive bonus system continued to hound me. After much discussion with my staff, I established a system like the one used to select officers for promotion in the U.S. Army. I had served on a couple of promotion selection boards in the Army Medical Department and was familiar with the process. The Army's system considered everyone fairly for promotion. Officers knew the criteria for selection, so it was up to the individual to prepare and meet the Army's standards to advance. Most significantly, the selection was based on results—it was based on their Officer Efficiency Reports.

The first step in the new selection process was to update the criteria to reduce bias. Next, we selected an evaluating team and developed score sheets and procedures. I wanted to create fair and more transparent evaluations that reduced bias and popularity votes. I also wanted selections based on measurable outcomes, i.e., specific and quantifiable results achieved because of their job performance.

The system I implemented was more formal than the existing system, but the adjustment was quick, and the process went smoothly. The secretary quickly accepted the new procedures. We published the results and were pleased when neither Congress nor the stakeholders complained.

I wish the system I developed had remained at the VA because the executive bonus scandals returned, with a vengeance, in future administrations. In 2007, four years after I left the position at the VA, the Subcommittee on Oversight and Investigations of the Committee on Veterans Affairs of the U.S. House of Representatives held a hearing about the senior executive bonuses at VA. There were reasons for concern. According to the committee's chair,

> The VA paid the highest average bonuses among all cabinet agencies. In 2006, 87 percent of senior executive service employees who were considered for bonuses received one. Central office bonuses averaged $4,000 more than field bonuses. Particularly in the central office, there appears to be a case of exaggerated Lake Wobegon Syndrome. Not only is everyone above average, almost everyone is outstanding. It appears that central office personnel are evaluated based on justifications written by the employees themselves, with no objective criteria factoring into the process. Indeed, it appears that bonuses to the central office were awarded primarily based on seniority and proximity to the secretary.[2]

CHALLENGING HEARSAY

Challenging all assertions was something I learned early in my military career. I put that maxim to work when a member of my staff briefed me about the imminent collapse of VACO's electronic payroll system. It was, in his words, being held together by "pins and needles," and the person who managed it was ill. As a result, employees at the VACO might not receive their checks on time. Something about the story didn't seem right, so I planned a secret trip to Austin to evaluate the situation.

When I arrived, I assembled the payroll staff in a large conference room and told them about the rumors I'd heard. The manager assured me the system was fine. I inquired about his health, and with a burst of hearty laughter, he indicated that he was in "top shape," and promised that everyone would be paid on time.

We continued to use the payroll system and experienced zero glitches or malfunctions. It appeared that someone had convinced one of my employees that the VACO needed to acquire a new payroll system. Had I not questioned my employee's assertion, we would have spent millions of dollars replacing a system that was fine.

At the VACO, I often served as the senior point of contact on matters related to Puerto Rico and the U.S. Virgin Islands. In 2001, I accompanied the VA secretary to Puerto Rico, Saint Thomas, and Saint Croix to visit VA facilities and discuss healthcare issues that impacted their veterans. During this trip, we discovered that the VA Hospital needed several upgrades. VA only had $50 million to upgrade a portion of the facility. To me, it made more sense to buy land and build a new hospital, so I started researching options.

During my next visit to Puerto Rico, I visited the Sabana Seca Naval Base. Scheduled for closure, the base included more than enough acreage for a new hospital and was only ten miles from the current VA Medical Center. There was so much space, it could also be used for a new cemetery, nursing home, and Veterans Benefits Administration office. Doing so would provide all VA benefits in one place for Puerto Rico and the Virgin Islands. We could also build an Emergency Operations Center in the new hospital for emergencies in the Caribbean.

I took the idea back to VACO. After much analysis, the cost made the project unfeasible. Although a new hospital was not built, my intervention was the catalyst for VA to subsequently build a new administration tower and infrastructure upgrades at the San Juan Medical Center.

A SAD DAY

My efforts at VA were interrupted on July 21, 2001, when I was at Dulles Airport on my way to visit my mother. Before departing, I received an anxious call from my brother in Puerto Rico. He told me that, after suddenly feeling ill, my mom had been taken to the hospital, where she passed away. Putting my hands over my ears, I closed my eyes tightly. I could not believe it. I had talked to her the night before, and she had sounded happy, surrounded by a group of ladies from her church and singing old church songs together. She'd told me she was looking forward to my visit. I was so devastated by the news that the flight to Puerto Rico seemed like an eternity.

I arrived in my hometown around noon, and my older brother was waiting for me. Together, we made the funeral arrangements with the help of a family friend who managed a local funeral home. My younger brother flew in from Milwaukee, Wisconsin, the following day, and we all planned a memorial service to be held in my mom's church. The days blurred together, and I was unable to sleep. My mom was the anchor of our family and someone I had always leaned on for support and encouragement.

I will never forget people silently filing into the church, stopping to shake our hands or give us hugs, and allowing us to share our grief with them. Some church members knew us when we were kids and attended Sunday Bible School there. Others were friends from my youth. Although the occasion was extremely solemn and sad, I renewed many old friendships.

The day after my mom's funeral, I returned to my office at VACO. Returning to work was emotionally challenging. I had to allow myself to grieve while trying to reestablish my work routine. A few days later, I received a letter of condolence from President Bush. It lifted my spirits and was an unexpected source of comfort.[3]

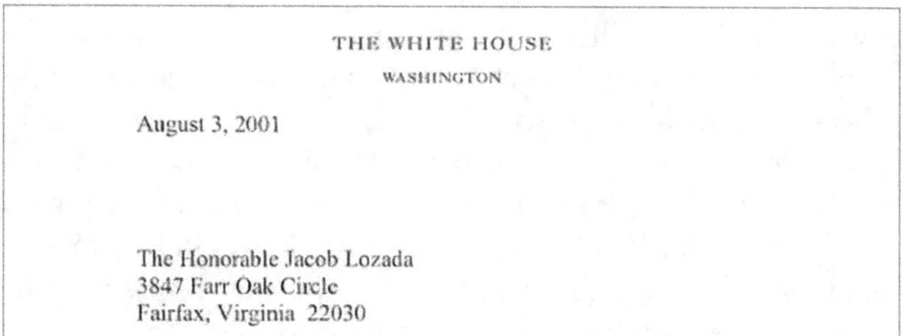

THE WHITE HOUSE

WASHINGTON

August 3, 2001

The Honorable Jacob Lozada
3847 Farr Oak Circle
Fairfax, Virginia 22030

Dear Dr. Lozada:

I am saddened to learn about your mother's passing. Although the days ahead will not be easy, I hope you will take comfort in the support of your family and friends.

Laura and I send our heartfelt sympathy. Our prayers are with you and your family at this difficult time.

Sincerely,

George W. Bush

Image 31. Letter of condolence from President Bush

SHOCK AND HORROR

On August 1, the president appointed me to the Task Force on Puerto Rico's Status.[4] As a U.S. territory, Puerto Rico was subject to U.S. laws, but it also exercised autonomy over local issues. The purpose of the task force was to provide options for the island's political status to the president. This appointment would soon become secondary to something far more serious.

On September 11, 2001, I was with VA leadership team members at a conference in San Diego. During one of our breaks, I saw two airplanes striking the Twin Towers on TV. Opening my mouth in disbelief, but not speaking, I was confused by what I was watching! I didn't know what was taking place until I heard the reports of two other hijacked planes heading into our nation's capital. I tried using my mobile phone, but it was partially disabled—it was impossible to communicate with my family or staff back in VACO. I knew my relatives in Puerto Rico would see the news and worry. They knew my office was near the White House, and they couldn't reach me to check on me.

As I watched the news, thousands of people walked the streets of Washington, DC, in a daze. Amid feelings of consternation, sadness, and anger, I felt a deeper sense of purpose and duty to our nation, which motivated me to continue to give back in the face of tragedy and help those affected.

Those of us in San Diego tried to return to Washington, DC, quickly, but to no avail. We requested military flights, but they had been heavily curtailed nationwide. Some VA executives rented a van and drove, arriving in Washington, DC, two days later. Others, like me, decided to stay at the hotel and wait.

After two days of waiting, I found a limited number of commercial flights; however, it took me all day and multiple stops to return home. I was exhausted physically and emotionally when I arrived, but at last, I was able to call my family and inform them that I was fine. The following day, when I arrived in my office, my employees were quieter; no one talked casually about their weekend plans anymore.

A few days later, the VA secretary appointed me to lead VA efforts to collect funds for September 11 victims. Working at a feverish pace, I planned the VA "Day of Giving" project which collected $316,252 to benefit the victims and their families.

September 11 shattered the nation's sense of security. To better coordinate security efforts across the federal government, the Department of Homeland Security was created. Stricter airport security measures were implemented, and training was conducted to ensure that the government agencies could perform their essential functions during emergencies. The federal government also took extra security measures, requiring everyone to show a valid identification and register prior to entering government buildings. Some agencies issued packets with emergency supplies, which had to be kept near one's desk. Others established security drills including "sheltering in place" measures. VA established a new organization to manage overall security and preparedness.

HONOR

In November, the Puerto Rican government invited me to an event to posthumously honor four Puerto Rican servicemen who had been awarded the Congressional Medal of Honor. During that event, they wanted to recognize me with a proclamation by their House of Representatives highlighting my extensive career. I was delighted to share this recognition with my family, friends, and the Veterans Service Organizations.

Image 32. The author with Puerto Rico's Veterans Service Organizations leaders and members of the House of Representatives, honoring the four Puerto Rican servicemen awarded the Congressional Medal of Honor

During this trip, a TV reporter met me at the airport with questions about the VA hospital in San Juan. Though she surprised me—I didn't know how she knew I was coming—I answered all her questions before running into two VA security officers who identified themselves as my "personal security detail." I'd never needed a security detail before, but they insisted, directing me to a government vehicle instead of a regular taxi. They drove me to my brother's house with a police escort and sirens.

As we turned onto his street, I saw him and his wife running outside to find out the cause of all the commotion. When the motorcycles and our vehicle stopped in front of them, several neighbors rushed out to find out what was going on. It took me a while to explain the reason for the police escort. I didn't feel comfortable having a security detail. It seemed excessive, but I appreciated the guards' support and dedication.

The following day, at the reception in the Capitol, my VACO staff set up a photo display of the Medal of Honor recipients. Each photo listed the individual's acts of heroism during combat. It was humbling to be recognized with those heroes. While I was in Puerto Rico, I also traveled to Humacao to attend another government event recognizing local veterans. Hundreds of local veterans attended, and I gave a short speech on the president's behalf.

MANY EVENTS

During my tenure at VA, I participated in many events on behalf of the VA and visited the White House several times.

Of the many events I attended, a few stand out.

- Acting as guest speaker at the 2002 Fourth of July celebration in San Juan, Puerto Rico and delivering a message from the president.

- Breakfast at the White House with HUD Secretary Mel Martínez and Deputy Assistant to the President Rubén Barrales.

- A reception at the Ronald Reagan Building and International Trade Center, where I met Secretary of State Colin Powell (a giant of a man).

- A reception at the White House to honor our nation's veterans and meeting the late Senator Bob Dole.

- Meeting Secretary of Defense Donald H. Rumsfeld at a White House reception.

- Pinning a VA pin to Martin Luther King III's lapel in my office during Black History Month.

Image 33. The author with Senator Bob Dole at the White House

The most memorable events, however, included President Bush. Watching the president assemble his management team (the cabinet and subcabinet appointees) at the Ronald Reagan Building and International Trade Center in Washington, DC, was very special. The president shared what had already been accomplished as well as his goals and expectations for the future.

As everyone fixed their eyes on the president, he leaned into us and said,

> "We came to Washington to set big goals, goals that will leave an indelible mark on the country after we leave. I think that it's important that as we implement our goals, it is vital that members of this administration be willing to challenge the status quo. So, one of the things we've got to do is focus on results. So, we're gonna lead, we are gonna achieve results and we are gonna do one more thing. We're gonna make Americans proud of what they see."[5]

The president's words about challenging the status quo, leaving an indelible mark, and focusing on results inspired me!

Following the president's remarks, Vice President Cheney, Secretaries Powell and Martinez, and Governor Whitman addressed those in attendance. Being among the nation's leaders was exhilarating.

Watching President Bush sign the House of Representatives Bill 1696 to expedite the construction of the World War II Memorial in the District of Columbia was also special. I was at Arlington National Cemetery on Memorial Day when he laid a wreath at the Tomb of the Unknown Soldier.

I also attended a reception at the White House to honor Professor Jaime Escalante, a Bolivian American high school *teacher* who taught calculus to high-achieving students from a poor Hispanic neighborhood in East Los Angeles. During this event, I had a short conversation with the president. Afraid my excitement would betray me, I chose my words carefully. Having the president's full attention for a moment was an amazing experience! I treasure a photo taken with President Bush during our conversation.

Image 34. The author with President George W. Bush at the White House

Image 35. Witnessing President Bush signing the World War II Memorial construction bill at the White House

Two Years

Most senior political appointees spend two to four years on the job. These positions are extremely demanding—days are long, and the pressures are relentless. Some appointees serve to enjoy the perks associated with these positions, enhancing their chances of landing a good job in the private sector, or using them as a starting point to transfer into a career position in the federal government. Others are appointed for supporting a presidential campaign. However, most appointees I knew—including me— wanted to make a difference, give back to the nation, and improve the federal government.

I considered it a great honor to be a member of the president's team, support our veterans, and improve the VA. I never intended to become a career federal employee, nor did I want to use my position to "pad my resume."

Among my many accomplishments during the two years I served at VA, some of my proudest were:

- Achieving a green score in the management of human capital under the President's Management Agenda. This agenda was a strategy to improve the management and performance of the federal government. Achieving a green score for the management of human capital was a big challenge. Because of my team's efforts, the U.S. Office of Personnel Management highlighted the VA for its promising human capital practices.

- Creating a new executive bonus system that received no complaints from either Congress or stakeholders. The existing system had been a source of considerable criticism. The VA, according to its critics, "suffered from a pervasive culture of awarding good performance evaluations and cash bonuses to its executives."

- Canceling the wasteful Human Resources Links (HRLinks) program. The VA had developed a highly controversial electronic human resources management system which had not produced the desired results. Even though many millions of dollars had been spent, HRLinks was not embraced by most of VA's senior leaders and specifically the VHA.

- Establishing a youth council in response to the challenge of an aging workforce.

- Creating two innovative internship programs for disadvantaged high school youth in San Antonio and Baltimore.

- Representing the president at various events in Puerto Rico and the mainland.

I enjoyed the challenges at the VA and the opportunity to serve our nation's veterans. However, after two years of highly intensive work, the environment turned toxic. My well-thought-out plans to modernize and reorganize human resources management could not get the required traction and support from top leadership. I also realized that "doing the right thing" was not a priority; maintaining the status quo and protecting bureaucratic fiefdoms was more important.

In February 2003, I prepared a short resignation letter, thanking the president for the opportunity to serve at the VA. After I signed it, I assembled my personal staff to deliver the news to them. When I informed them of my decision, the room went silent. I recounted our accomplishments and thanked them for their support. When the deputy secretary learned of my departure, he offered me a senior advisor position at the U.S. Office of Personnel Management. I told him I would consider the job offer.

RECOGNITION

A week prior to leaving the VA, the secretary announced a farewell award ceremony for me at the VACO Conference Center. I appreciated the gesture because other senior political appointees had left the VA without such a ceremony. The day of the event, the secretary and deputy secretary, top VA executives, my staff, representatives of the VSOs, and many VACO employees were present. Having so many people show up to honor me was a humbling experience. One senior executive shook my hand and said, "Dr. Lozada, thank you for your service at VA. You always did the right thing."

During the ceremony, the secretary presented me with an encased flag with the VA coat of arms and four stars, symbolizing my rank as assistant secretary. That flag had been on display in my office since my swearing-in. Before the ceremony ended, the secretary presented me with the highest award the VA bestows: the Department of Veterans Affairs Exceptional Service Award. The award caught me by surprise because it is typically given at retirement or for many years of service—I had only been at the VA for two years.

I experienced a mix of emotions that day: extreme gratitude to the president for giving me the once-in-a-lifetime opportunity to serve on his leadership team, appreciation to the people who supported me and helped me, and validation that my work and abilities were recognized and valued.

Image 36. The author receiving the Department of Veterans Affairs Exceptional Service Award and flag during his farewell ceremony

On February 4, 2003, I received a letter of appreciation from the chief of staff to the president. I was touched by his gesture and generosity.

CHIEF OF STAFF TO THE PRESIDENT
THE WHITE HOUSE

February 4, 2003

The Honorable Jacob Lozada
3847 Farr Oak Circle
Fairfax, VA 22030

Dear Jacob:

Thank you for your continued hard work and fine service as a key
member of this Administration. Enclosed is a commemorative copy
of the President's State of the Union Address, delivered to Congress
on January 29, 2003. In it, the President outlines his agenda for the
coming year and his vision for a better, safer, more compassionate
America.

With the President's and the Vice President's leadership, and the
hard work of a dedicated team, we will meet the goals outlined in
this historic speech.

Sincerely,

Andrew H. Card, Jr.

Enclosure

Thank you!

Image 37. Letter of appreciation from the chief of staff to the president

At this stage of my professional career, my hard work
and the many sacrifices I had made since my early childhood
in Puerto Rico had been fully rewarded. I had achieved top
leadership positions as a colonel in the U.S. Army, principal and
managing consultant in two private sector consulting firms, and
as an assistant secretary nominated by a U.S. president and fully

confirmed by the U.S. Senate. The time had arrived for me to give back via the not-for-profit sector.

I used my talents and experience to serve a variety of organizations that touched my heart. During the second half of 2003, I cofounded and became the first president of the Association of University of Puerto Rico Alumni and Friends Abroad (UPRAA). Since its inception, UPRAA has awarded over $300,000 in scholarships to students with financial need. In 2007, I was selected for the AARP National Board of Directors (the first Puerto Rican to be so honored), and in 2008 I began my service on the Medical Musical Group Chorale and Symphony Orchestra board of directors.

In 2011, I was appointed by President Barack Obama as a member of the Advisory Group on Prevention, Health Promotion, and Integrative and Public Health. In 2017, the governor of Puerto Rico appointed me as a member of the "Frente por Puerto Rico" (a group of Puerto Rican leaders including former governors to advocate for the island's economic recovery), and in 2018 I was chosen to serve as chair of the Supervisory Committee of Andrews Federal Credit Union.

Finding Love Again

In 2020, a neighbor introduced me to a lady born in Puerto Rico but reared in the mainland. She worked as a dental assistant in his dental practice in Fairfax, Virginia. When I called her, we talked for several hours and found that our values, life goals, and beliefs aligned. Like me, she enjoyed traveling, working out, and trekking. On our first dinner date, we connected instantly. I was entranced by her personality, big smile, and care for others. We got on great, talking for hours. We fell in love quite quickly after that! As we got to know each other, we agreed that our common goal was to build a relationship that would bring us joy, satisfaction, and a sense of partnership. We wanted to be happy, enjoy life together, and support each other. After several months of dating, we decided to move to Austin, Texas, and get married—one of the best days of my life. I am extremely happy and thankful for Clary coming into my life.

Life's Lessons

Throughout my life's journey, I have learned many important lessons that I believe are the keys to success. The top ten most valuable lessons I've learned are:

1. Challenge all assertions.
2. Never assume the victim's role.
3. Your vision must be stronger than your current reality.
4. Luck favors the prepared mind.
5. Set the highest standards for yourself and others.
6. Cultivate mentoring relationships.
7. In ninety-nine percent of cases, culture trumps strategy.
8. Be all you can be.
9. Stay grounded in your past—cherish your upbringing.
10. Never take no for an answer—PERSIST!

When I left Puerto Rico—a twenty-two-year-old eager to fulfill my two-year U.S. Army obligation—little did I know of the challenges I would face and the opportunities that would come my way. Luckily, I lived in a nation full of opportunities. A nation where achieving the American Dream was and continues to be a reachable goal to those who work hard, establish a strong vision for themselves, and persevere. A nation that would provide the opportunities for a humble kid, born and raised in public housing in Puerto Rico, to achieve his dreams and aspirations and succeed.

ABOUT THE AUTHOR

Dr. Jacob Lozada is a man of faith who values God, his family, his nation, and his friends. His faith was imbued in him by his mother at an early age. She also instilled in him the importance of character and personal values. His father, who always saw America as the greatest nation on earth, inspired Jacob's love for his country.

Among his many honors and recognitions, Dr. Jacob Lozada has been profiled by *Hispanic Business Magazine* as one of the 100 Most Influential Hispanics and by *National Journal* as one of Washington's Decision Makers. He was also appointed Principal of the Council for Excellence in Government and adjunct assistant professor at The George Washington University.

He is the recipient of the League of United Latin American Citizens' Presidential Citation; the American G.I. Forum Founder's Award; the U.S. Army Baylor Program in Healthcare Administration and the University of Puerto Rico at Humacao's

Distinguished Alumni Awards. He is also the recipient of a special proclamation from the interim governor of Puerto Rico, Baltasar Corrada del Río, recognizing his retirement from the U.S. Army; three proclamations from the House of Representatives and the Senate of Puerto Rico for his appointment as assistant secretary at the VA; and one proclamation from the mayor of his hometown of San Lorenzo, Puerto Rico in recognition of his public service.

His military awards include the Legion of Merit, six Army Meritorious Service Medals, the Defense Meritorious Service Medal, two Army Commendation Medals, the Order of Military Medical Merit, and the Expert Field Medical Badge.

Jacob is passionate about being a role model and mentor to young adults. He's helped raise funds for scholarships for Puerto Rican students, and for several years he funded a summer school for underprivileged students in Humacao, Puerto Rico.

Traveling, trekking, and watching his grandson Luca's basketball games have now become his favorite pastimes. In 2014, he and his son Jason completed the Camino de Santiago in Spain (a 70.8-mile medieval pilgrimage that dates back over 1,100 years). Most recently, he hiked the Argentine and Chilean Patagonia.

Jacob's daughter Valerie resides in Colorado with her husband Steven. His son Jason resides in Texas with his wife Lili and sons Carlo and Luca. He remains close with his brothers and half-sister, Juan Manuel, Elías, and Carmen. Jacob resides in Austin, Texas, with his wife Clary.

Email: jacoblozada052@gmail.com

ENDNOTES

NOTES TO INTRODUCTION

1. "Ellis Island Medals of Honor Yearbook," *Medal Yearbook* (Token Publishing Ltd., 2018), 1.

NOTES TO CHAPTER 2

1. General view of the bridge, the river, and an old segment of the San Lorenzo – Las Piedras highway from the north - Puente de la Marina, San Lorenzo-Florida & Cerro Gordo Neighborhoods, spanning Rio Grande de Loiza River at Narciso Varona-Suarez Street, San Lorenzo, San Lorenzo Municipio, PR Photos from Survey HAER PR-38 https://www.loc.gov/resource/hhh.pr1496.photos/?sp=1.

NOTES TO CHAPTER 4

1. Department of the Army, DA Form 67-5, U.S. Army Officer Efficiency Report, February 2, 1967.
2. Department of the Army, Headquarters, 2nd Battalion, The U.S. Army Medical Training Center, Fort Sam Houston Texas, Letter, August 2, 1968.
3. Department of the Army, Headquarters, Valley Forge General Hospital, Letter of Commendation, May 23, 1973.

NOTES TO CHAPTER 5

1. Department of the Army, DA Form 1059, Service School Academic Evaluation Report, September 26, 1978.
2. Order of Military Medical Merit, PO Box 340097, Fort Sam Houston, Texas, Letter, March 18, 1987.
3. Office of the Commandant, Academy of Health Sciences, Fort Sam Houston, Texas, Letter, May 3, 1989.

4. Commander 8th Personnel Command, ATTN: EAPC-PF-M APO SF 96301, Letter, September 6, 1989.
5. Department of the Army, HQDA (DASG-MS) 5109 Leesburg Pike, Falls Church, VA 22041, Letter, September 15, 1989.

Notes to Chapter 7

1. U.S. Newswire, 202-347-2770/President to nominate Lozada and Scalia to Administration, April 25, 2001.
2. Leonor Mulero, *El Nuevo Día*, "Nomina George Bush a un puertorriqueño." Translated: "Bush Nominates a Puerto Rican," May 2, 2001.

Notes to Chapter 8

1. U.S. Senate Committee on Veterans Affairs, Washington, DC 20510, Letter, May 9, 2001.
2. The White House, *Memorandum for Cabinet Members and Agency Heads, Subject: Employment Guidelines for Potential Appointees,* January 26, 2001.
3. The White House, Washington, DC, Memorandum from Deputy Assistant to the President for Legislative Affairs, May 11, 2001.
4. Committee on Veterans Affairs, U.S. Senate Hearings on various Presidential nominations for the Department of Veterans Affairs, U.S. Senate, May 16, 2001.
5. Ibid.
6. Sila M. Calderón, Governor of Puerto Rico, Letter to the author, June 4, 2001.
7. *El Nuevo Día*, "Satisfecha Sila por nombramiento de Lozada." Translated: "Sila (the Governor of Puerto Rico) Is Satisfied with Lozada's Nomination," June 6, 2001.

Notes to Chapter 9

1. Ozzie García, Dallas Office of Public Affairs (OPA), *"Eager to learn – 53 Texas high school students got an introduction to public service and more this summer through an innovative program,"* p. 6.
2. Committee on Veterans Affairs, U.S. House of Representatives, One Hundred Tenth Congress, First Session, *Senior Executive Bonuses: Ensuring the U.S. Department of Veterans Affairs Process Works,* Hearing before the Subcommittee on Oversight and Investigations

U.S. Government Printing Office, Serial Number 110-26, June 12, 2007.

3. President George W. Bush, Letter, August 3, 2001.

4. Mildred Rivera Marrero, "Ashcroft y Barrales a trabajar con el status." Translated: "Ashcroft and Barrales to Work on the Status," *El Nuevo Día*, August 2, 2001, p. 3.

5. https://georgewbush-whitehouse.archives.gov/results/leadership/feb13transcript.html

ACKNOWLEDGMENTS

I am hugely grateful for the continuous support and love given to me throughout the years by members of my family. Their loyalty and love have inspired me.

I am also thankful to my public school teachers in Puerto Rico and my mentors during my Army career. They helped me grow as a student, military officer, and leader. They also made me a better person.

I would like to express my gratitude to my many friends in Puerto Rico and the mainland. I am also indebted to those who supported me in the private sector, during my service as a presidential appointee, and during my nonprofit work.

Lastly, I want to thank those who encouraged me to tell my life's story by writing this book and spurred me on to continue writing.